# SPAIN AND PORTUGAL IN YOUR POCKET

# SPAIN AND PORTUGAL
## IN YOUR
## POCKET

A STEP-BY-STEP GUIDE
AND TRAVEL ITINERARY

BY RICK STEVES
AND MICHAEL MULLER,
CORNELIA STAUCH AND
WOLFGANG ABEL

Northcote House

**British Library Cataloguing in Publication Data**

Steves, Rick, *1955–*
    Spain and Portugal in your pocket: a step-by step guide and
    travel itinerary.—UK ed.—(Pocket travellers).
    1. Spain—Visitors' guides. 2. Portugal—Visitors' guides
    I. Title Steves, Rick, *1955–* Spain and Portugal in 22 days III.
    Series
    914.6'0483

    ISBN 1-85373-090-4

**Maps** Jim Wood

This edition first published in 1988 by Northcote House Publishers
Ltd, Harper & Row House, Estover Road, Plymouth PL6 7PZ,
United Kingdom. Tel: Plymouth (0752) 705251. Telex: 45635.
Fax: (0752) 777603.

Printed and bound in Great Britain by
Richard Clay Ltd, Bungay, Suffolk

# CONTENTS

How to Use This Book                                          7
Back Door Travel Philosophy                                  12
Itinerary                                                    13
Helpful Hints                                                17
Tour 1    Arrive in Madrid                                   18
Tour 2    Madrid                                             23
Tour 3    Madrid and Side Trips                              26
Tour 4    Madrid — Segovia — Salamanca                       28
Tour 5    Salamanca — Coimbra                                33
Tour 6    Coimbra — Sao Martinho do Porto                    37
Tour 7    Beach Time and Circular Excursion                  40
Tour 8    Sao Martinho — Obidos — Lisbon                     42
Tour 9    Lisbon                                             48
Tour 10   The Art and History of Lisbon                      50
Tour 11   Side Trips from Lisbon                             53
Tour 12   Lisbon — Evora — Interior — Algarve               56
Tour 13   Salema, Your Algarve Hideaway                      59
Tour 14   Side Trip to Sagres                                60
Tour 15   The Drive to Seville                               61
Tour 16   Seville                                            64
Tour 17   Seville — Andalucian Villages — Ronda             67
Tour 18   Ronda to the Costa del Sol                         72
Tour 19   Granada                                            75
Tour 20   Granada to Toledo                                  80
Tour 21   Toledo, Return to Madrid                           83
Post-Tour Options
    Barcelona                                                86
    Galicia — The Other Spain                                88
    Santiago de Compostela                                   90
    The Azores                                               93
    Morocco                                                  94
Iberian History                                              99
Art and Architecture                                        101
Bullfighting                                                103
Spanish Cuisine                                             104
Portuguese Cuisine                                          109
Accommodation                                               111
Transport                                                   113
Language                                                    117
Hours, Siestas and Fiestas                                  123
Basic Information                                            126

**Spain and Portugal**

# HOW TO USE THIS BOOK

This book is the tour guide in your pocket. It lets you be the boss by giving you the best basic itinerary in Spain and Portugal and a suggested way to use each day most efficiently. It is for do-it-youselfers — with or without a tour.

This series originated (and is still used) as the tour handbook for those who join Rick on his 'Back Door Europe' Tours. Since most large organised tours work to keep their masses ignorant while visiting many of the same places we'll cover, this book is vital to anyone who hopes to maintain independence and flexibility while taking a typical big coach tour.

Realistically, most travellers are interested in the predictable biggies — Alhambra, Prado and flamenco. This tour covers those while mixing in a good dose of 'back door' intimacy with Andalucian hilltowns, forgotten Algarve fishing villages and desolate La Mancha windmills.

While the trip is designed as a car tour, it also makes a great train/bus trip. Each day's journey is adapted for train and bus travel with explanations, options and appropriate schedules included.

The trip starts and ends in Madrid, but you may consider flying into Lisbon and out of Madrid (or vice-versa). Your travel agent will advise you on the best, and cheapest, way of doing this. To adjust your itinerary for this plan, you'd probably skip a few cities in the north and visit others as side trips from Madrid and Lisbon. The saving in driving time you get from doing it this way gives you more time for some of the post-tour options.

A three-week car hire (split two ways) or a three-week first class Eurailpass costs £200 ($350) at the time of writing. For room and board reckon on about £12 ($20) a day for 21 days, totalling some £250 ($440). This is a feasible budget if you know the tricks — see *Europe Through the Back Door*. Add £175 ($300) fun money and you've got yourself a great Iberian adventure for £625 ($1,100) plus the cost of getting there. Do it!

Of course, connect-the-dots travel isn't perfect, just as colour-by-numbers isn't good art. But this book is your friendly fisherman, your Spaniard in a jam, your handbook. It's a well-thought-out and tested itinerary. We've done it on our own and with groups. Use it, take advantage of it, but don't let it rule you.

Try to travel outside peak season — anytime but June 20 to August 20 — so finding hotels won't be a problem; wear a moneybelt; use local tourist information centres, and don't be a typical tourist.

This book should be read through completely before your trip, and then used as a rack to hang more ideas on. As you study and travel and plan and talk to people you'll fill it with notes. It's your tool.

The book is completely modular and is adaptable to any Iberian trip. You'll find 21 units (tours) — or days — each built with the same sections:

1. **Introductory overview** of the tour.
2. An hour-by-hour **Suggested schedule** that we recommend for each tour.
3. List of the most important **Sightseeing highlights** (rated: ● ● ● Don't miss; ● ● Try hard to see; ● Worthwhile if you can make it).
4. **Transport** plan for drivers; plus an adapted plan with schedules for train and bus travellers.
5. **Food** and **accommodation**: How and where to find the best budget places, including addresses, phone numbers, and our favourites.
6. **Helpful hints** on orientation, shopping, transport, day-to-day chores.
7. An easy-to-read **map** locating all recommended places.
8. **Itinerary options** for those with more or less than the suggested time, or with particular interests. This itinerary is *rubbery*.

At the back of the book, we've included some post-tour options if you have more time. There's also a thumbnail sketch of Spanish and Portuguese culture, history, art, food and language, as well as lists of festivals, foreign phrases and other helpful information.

## Efficient travellers think ahead

This itinerary assumes you are a well-organised traveller who lays departure groundwork upon arrival. Read this entire book before you leave and then read a day ahead. Keep a list of all the things that should be taken care of and ward off problems whenever possible before they happen.

This itinerary also assumes that if you were always that well-organised, you'd be Chairman of ICI and wouldn't *need* a budget guidebook. Therefore, we've scheduled in some slack time to account for unanticipated problems. Do your best!

## When to go

Peak season (July and August) is most crowded, hot, and difficult. During this time it's best to arrive early and phone hotels in advance (phone from one hotel to the next; your receptionist can help you). Things like banking, laundry stops, good mail days and picnics should be anticipated and planned

for. If you expect to travel smart, you will. If you insist on being
confused, your trip will be a mess.

## Prices

For simplicity, we've priced things throughout this book in round
figures (pounds and dollars). Prices, as well as hours, telephone
numbers and so on, are always changing and I have tossed timidity
out of the window knowing you'll understand that this book, like any
guidebook, starts growing old before it's even printed. Please don't
expect Spain and Portugal to have stood entirely still since this book
was written, and do what you can to phone ahead or doublecheck
hours and times when you arrive.

Our listings cover travellers with daily room and board budgets
ranging from £10 ($15) to £25 ($40). The room rates we quote are
for doubles (usually without private shower and with breakfast).
Singles generally cost one-third less than a double. Triples and quads
are plentiful and cheaper per person.

## Scheduling

Your overall itinerary strategy is a fun challenge. Read through this
book and note the problem days: Mondays, when many museums are
closed, and Sundays when public transport is meagre. Saturdays are
virtually weekdays. It's good to mix intense and relaxed periods.
Every trip needs at least a few slack days. While this plan works (we
get piles of postcards from travelling readers), for some the pace is
hectic. Our goal has been maximum thrills at a reasonable tempo.
Skip things or add days according to your travel style.

Train travellers should realise that "the trains in Spain mainly are a
pain", making the full itinerary virtually impossible. Be prepared to
streamline with overnight train rides, skip some out-of-the-way places
and take a slower pace.

## Keeping up with the news (if you must)

To keep in touch with world news while travelling in Europe, we use
the *International Herald Tribune* which comes out almost daily via
satellite. Every Tuesday the European editions of *Time* and *Newsweek*
hit the stands. They are full of articles of particular interest to
European travellers. Some UK papers are available in major cities.
News in English is only available where there's enough demand — in
big cities and tourist centres.

## Recommended guidebooks

This small book is your itinerary handbook. To really enjoy and
appreciate these busy weeks, you'll also need some directory-type
guidebook information. It may hurt to spend £18 ($30) or £25 ($40)
on extra guidebooks, but when you consider the improvements they
will make to your holiday — not to mention the money they'll save

you — *not* buying them would be perfectly "penny-wise and pound foolish". Here is our recommended guidebook strategy.

**General low-budget directory-type guidebook** — You need one. The best we've found are *Let's Go: Spain, Portugal and Morocco* (Columbus Books, London) and the *Rough Guides* to Spain and Portugal. *Let's Go* is updated each year and is a spinoff of the wonderful *Let's Go: Europe* guidebook. Its approach is rather hip and youthful, and if you've got £15 ($25) a day for room and board you may be a little rich for some of its info but, especially if you're going to Morocco, it's the best info source around.

Mark Ellingham has written very practical *Rough Guides* to both Spain and Portugal, published by Routledge & Kegan Paul, London. He has an excellent command of both cultures and a wealth of good info. They are not as fresh as *Let's Go* which is updated annually.

Older travellers like the style of Arthur Frommer's *Spain and Portugal on $20 a Day*, but neither it nor Fodor's is very practical.

**Cultural and sightseeing guides** — Michelin's *Green Guides* for Spain and Portugal are both great for info on the sights and culture (nothing on room and board). These are written with the driver in mind (on Michelin tyres of course). The new *American Express Guide to Spain* (by Mitchell Beazley) is also good. The encyclopaedic Blue Guides to Spain and Portugal are dry and scholastic but just right for some people.

**Maps** — Michelin makes the best. Available and inexpensive throughout Iberia.

**Phrase book** — *Berlitz Spanish Phrase Book*, £2.25.

**Rick Steves' books** — Finally, we've written this book assuming you've read or will read the latest edition of Rick Steves' book on the skills of budget travel, *Europe Through the Back Door*. To keep this book small and pocket-sized, we've resisted the temptation to repeat the most applicable and important information already included in *Europe Through the Back Door*; there is no overlap.

*Europe Through the Back Door* gives you the basic skills, the foundation which makes this demanding itinerary possible. There are chapters on minimising jet lag, packing light, driving or train travel, finding budget beds without reservations, changing money, theft and the tourist, hurdling the language barrier, health, travel photography, long-distance telephoning in Europe, travellers' toilet trauma, laundry, and itinerary strategies and techniques that are so very important.

Rick's *Europe 101* gives you the story of Europe's people, history and art and would be a helpful preparation for this trip. Your bookshop should have these two books or you can get them direct from Northcote House Publishers, address on the back cover.

## Books we would buy for this trip

(1) *Let's Go: Spain and Portugal* (rip out appropriate chapters)
(2) *Berlitz Spanish Phrase Book*, (3) *Michelin's Green Guides* for
Spain and Portugal.

Read *Europe Through the Back Door* and *Europe 101* at home
before departing.

Apart from books, a traveller's best friends are the tourist
offices you'll find throughout Spain and Portugal. Use them — for
maps, accommodation, where to find a pharmacy, driving
instructions, recommendations for night life, etc.

## Freedom

Our goal with this book is to free you, not chain you. Please
defend your spontaneity like you would your mother, and use this
book to avoid time- and money-wasting mistakes, to get more
intimate with Iberia by travelling as a temporary local person,
and as a point of departure from which to shape your best
possible travel experience.

Be confident, enjoy the hills and the valleys, and *Buen viaje!*

## BACK DOOR TRAVEL PHILOSOPHY

# AS TAUGHT IN EUROPE THROUGH THE BACK DOOR

*Travel is intensified living — maximum thrills per minute and one of the last great sources of legal adventure. In many ways, the less you spend the more you get.*

*Experiencing the real thing requires candid informality — going "Through the Back Door".*

*Affording travel is a matter of priorities. Many people who "can't afford a trip" could sell their cars and travel for two years.*

*You can travel anywhere in the world for £15 ($20) a day plus transport costs. Money has little to do with enjoying your trip. In fact, spending more money builds a thicker wall between you and what you came to see.*

*A tight budget forces you to travel "close to the ground", meeting and communicating with the people, not relying on service with a purchased smile. Never sacrifice sleep, nutrition, safety or cleanliness in the name of budget. Simply enjoy the local-style alternatives to expensive hotels and restaurants.*

*Extroverts have more fun. If your trip is low on magic moments, kick yourself and start making things happen. Dignity and good travel don't mix.*

*If you don't enjoy a place, it's often because you don't know enough about it. Seek out the truth. Recognise tourist traps.*

*A culture is legitimised by its existence. Give a people the benefit of your open mind. Think of things as different but not better or worse.*

*Of course, travel, like the world, is a series of hills and valleys. Be fanatically positive and militantly optimistic.*

*Travel is addictive. It can make you a happier person, as well as a citizen of the world. Our Earth is home to five billion equally important people. That's wonderfully humbling.*

*Globetrotting destroys ethnocentricity and encourages the understanding and appreciation of various cultures. Travel changes people. Many travellers toss aside their "hometown blinkers", assimilating the best points of different cultures into their own character.*

*The world is a cultural garden. We're working on the ultimate salad. Won't you join us?*

**Tour Route**

# ITINERARY

**TOUR 1** Arrive in Madrid, catch bus or taxi to Puerta del Sol to find your hotel. Get your bearings with an easy afternoon and evening. Possible stroll around old town.

**TOUR 2** Today we dive headlong into the grandeur of Spain's past, spending the morning at the lavish Royal Palace. After lunch and a siesta in the giant Retiro Park, we'll cover the canvas highlights of the Prado museum and Picasso's Guernica. Culture shock will lower its sleepy boom early this evening.

**TOUR 3** Spend the morning browsing through Madrid's old quarter and maybe the huge flea market. The afternoon is free for a bullfight, a side trip to El Escorial, or shopping. We'll spend the evening in the busy Malasña quarter dining late like Spain does. (This is one of 3 easy-to-cut tours on this itinerary).

**TOUR 4** We'll pick up our hired car first thing this morning (or catch the train) and head for historic Segovia where we'll have four hours to tour its impressive Roman aqueduct, cathedral, and Alcazar fortress. After a few hours on the road we'll arrive in Salamanca in time to join the paseo (city stroll) and linger over dinner on Spain's greatest square, the Plaza Mayor.

**TOUR 5** Spend the morning exploring the old town and Salamanca's venerable university. Drive for about an hour for lunch in the walled frontier town of Ciudad Rodrigo and then cross into Portugal, driving through its wildly natural countryside to Coimbra in time to find a hotel and enjoy a dinner in the old quarter.

**TOUR 6** Spend the morning enjoying the historic centre of what was the Portuguese capital when the Moors held Lisbon. After touring the university — Portugal's Oxford — have lunch and drive south for two hours to Batalha, the country's greatest church and a 600 year old symbol of its independence from Spain. The fishing village of São Martinho is nearby. Find a room and enjoy dinner on the Atlantic coast.

**TOUR 7** There's plenty to do during a circular morning excursion to small towns. After visiting a wine museum and the Alcobaca monastery we'll be ready for lunch in Nazare — a fishing village turned holiday camp. The afternoon and evening are free to explore Nazare, soak up some sun, take a swim, sample today's catch for dinner and watch the sun dive into the sea in Nazare or in our village base of São Martinho.

**TOUR 8** After breakfast we'll drive to Obidos — Portugal's medieval walled gem town — for a wander. Some of Portugal's most famous seafood is ours for lunch and we should be in Lisbon by 4:00. The salty Alfama quarter is a great place for an evening stroll and dinner.

**TOUR 9** This day in Lisbon is for relaxing, shopping and getting orientated. Spend the morning in the fashionable old Baixa and Chiado quarters shopping and people-watching. After lunch we'll enjoy the best view in town from the castle and walk through the noisy nooks and cobbled crannies of the incredibly atmospheric Alfamas sailors' district. We'll finish the day with drinking and droning in a melancholy Fado restaurant.

**TOUR 10** Now we'll get into Lisbon's history and art. The morning will be busy enjoying 2,000 exciting years of art in the Gulbenkian Museum. After lunch we'll head out to the suburb of Belem for a good look at the wonders of Portugal's Golden Age — the huge Monument to the Discoveries, the Belem tower and the great Manueline-style church and cloisters.

**TOUR 11** Today we make a circular trip from Lisbon. First to Sintra with its hill-capping fairy-tale Pena Palace and the mysterious and desolate ruined Moorish castle. Then on to the wild and windy Capo da Roca. From this western-most point in Europe we go to the stately resort town of Cascaís for dinner and an hour on the noble beachfront promenade.

**TOUR 12** Today we leave early for Evora, where we'll spend a few hours exploring and having lunch. The afternoon will be spent driving from remote village to village south through the vast Alentejo region. By dinnertime we should be in our Algarve hideaway — the tiny fishing village of Salema.

**TOUR 13** This is our "holiday from the holiday" day, with beach time and fun in the Algarve sun.

**TOUR 14** A day to explore Portugal's south coast. After an elegant *pousada* breakfast, we'll drive to Cape Sagres, Europe's "Land's End" and home of Henry the Navigator's famous navigation school. Spend the afternoon and evening in the jet-setty resort of Portimão or return to the peace and sleepy beauty of Salema.

**TOUR 15** Leave early, driving across the entire Algarve with a few stops. By mid-afternoon you'll be on the tiny ferry, crossing the river to Spain where you're just two hours from Seville.

**TOUR 16** Today is for exciting Seville. After a busy morning in the Alcazar, Moorish garden, cathedral, climbing the Giralda Tower and exploring the old Jewish quarter, you'll need a peaceful lunch on the river and a siesta in the shady Maria Louisa Park. Spend the late afternoon browsing through the shopping district and visiting the Weeping Virgin altarpiece. Seville is Spain's late-night capital — get swallowed up in the ritual paseo and finish things off with dinner and a flamenco show in the Santa Cruz district.

**TOUR 17** We'll leave Seville early and arrive in Ronda late, filling this day with as much small town adventure as possible as we explore the Ruta de Pueblos Blancos — route of the white villages. The Andalucian interior is dotted with friendly and forgotten little white-washed towns.

**TOUR 18** After a morning to enjoy gorge-straddling Ronda's old town and bullring, we'll leave the rugged interior for the famous beach resorts of the Costa del Sol. We'll spend half a day on the coast not to enjoy the beach and sun as much as to experience a social phenomenon — the devastation of a beautiful coastline by sun-worshipping human beings. The headquarters you choose will depend on the atmosphere you want — hip, aristocrat, package-tour-tacky or quiet.

**TOUR 19** Escape very early to arrive in Granada by 9:00am. Spend most of the day in the great Moorish Alhambra palace with a picnic lunch in the royal Generalife gardens. Evenings are best spent exploring Spain's best old Moorish quarter, the Albaicin. This is a great place for dinner and an Alhambra view.

**TOUR 20** Drive all day to Toledo stopping for lunch in La Mancha, Don Quixote country. Find accommodation in the medieval depths of Toledo — Spain's best preserved and most historic city. An atmospheric (and delicious) roast suckling pig dinner is a great way to end the day.

**TOUR 21** Toledo has so much to see. Today we'll tour Spain's greatest cathedral and enjoy the greatest collections of El Greco paintings anywhere. Our tour ends tonight as we drive back to Madrid, return the car and check into the same hotel we stayed in when we began 21 days ago.

## HELPFUL HINTS

Phone before going to the airport to confirm departure time as scheduled. Bring something to do — a book, a journal, some handwork — and make any waits and delays easy on yourself. Remember, no matter how long it takes, it is worth it! If you arrived in one piece on the day you hoped to, the trip was a smashing success.

**To minimise jet lag** (body clock adjustment, stress) if flying a long distance:
● Leave well rested. Pretend you are leaving a day earlier than you really are. Plan accordingly and enjoy a peaceful last day.
● Minimise stress during the flight by eating lightly, avoiding alcohol, caffeine and sugar. Drink juice.
● Sleep through the in-flight movie — or at least close your eyes and pretend to.

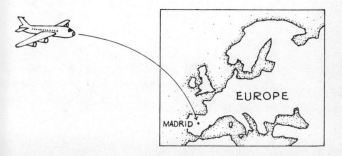

## TOUR 1

## ARRIVE IN MADRID!

Try to arrange things so that you arrive in the morning.
That way, you have time to orientate yourself. Today will
be spent getting acquainted with Madrid and finding a
room for your three-night stay.

### Suggested Schedule

Arrive at Madrid airport or station.
Take bus, metro or taxi into town.
Find hotel room.
Late dinner (in the Spanish tradition), relax.

Madrid's Barajas Airport is 10 miles east of the city centre. Like
most European airports, it has a bank that keeps long hours and
offers fair exchange rates. There are also a tourist info desk
(English speaking, helpful, free Madrid map, room info), on-the-
spot car hire agencies, and easy public transport into town.

Airport taxis are notoriously expensive. Take the yellow bus
into Madrid. It leaves about 4 times an hour for Plaza Colón (£1
($1.50), 20-min. journey).

If you're arriving by train from France or Barcelona, you'll
arrive at the modern Chamartin station. While you're at the
station, make a reservation for your departure. Then catch the
metro (requiring one change of lines) to metro stop 'Sol'. Taxis
are reasonable from the station.

Car hire: If at all possible, don't drive in Madrid. Hire your car
when you're ready to leave. Ideally, have that arranged through
your travel agent at home. In Madrid try Europacar (García de
Paredes 12), Hertz (Gran Vía 80) or Avis (Gran Vía 60).

### Orientation

Madrid is the hub of Spain. This modern capital of 4 million is
young by European standards. Only 400 years ago, King Philip II
decided to make it the capital of his empire. One hundred years
ago Madrid had only 300,000 people, so while nine-tenths of the
city is modern sprawl, the historical centre can be covered easily
on foot.

The Puerta de Sol is dead centre. In fact, this is even
considered the centre of Spain — notice the kilometre 0 marker at
the police station from which all of Spain is surveyed. An east-

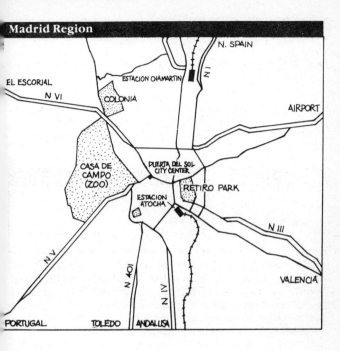

**Madrid Region**

west axis from the Royal Palace to the Prado Museum and Retiro Park cuts the historic centre in half.

North of the Puerto del Sol in the commercial street, the Gran Vía, runs east and west. Between the Gran Vía and the Puerta del Sol are pedestrian shopping streets. The Grand Vía, bubbling with business, expensive shops, and cinemas, leads down to the impressively modern Plaza de España. North of the Gran Vía is the fascinating Malasaña quarter with its colourful small houses, shoemakers' shops, milk vendors, bars, and cheap hotels. The Plaza Dos de Mayo hosts a lively scene each night.

To the southwest of the Puerta del Sol is an older district (16th century) with the great Plaza Mayor and plenty of relics from pre-industrial Spain. In the Lavapies quarter (southeast of Plaza Mayor) notice the names of the streets: Calles de Cuchilleros (knife smiths), Laterones (brass-casters), Bordaderos (embroiderers), Tinteros (dyers), Curtideros (tanners).

East of the Puerta del Sol is Madrid's huge museum (Prado), huge park (Retiro), and tiny river (Manzanares). Just north of the park is the elegant Salamanca quarter.

## Accommodation

Madrid has plenty of centrally located budget hotels and
pensions. Taxis are cheap. Upon arrival in the city centre, I'd take
one to Puerta del Sol and wander generally south and east.
Doorbells line each building entrance. Push one that says
'pension'. You'll have no trouble finding a decent double for £7-12
($12-20).

Choose small streets. The rooms get cheaper — and seedier —
as you approach the Atocha station. Hotels on Gran Vía are more
expensive and less atmospheric, but are still good value.

**Hostal Miami**, clean, quiet and central (Gran Vía 44, tel.
521-14-64, £8 ($13)) is like staying at an eccentric aunt's in a
seaside resort with its plastic flower decor and bubbly landlady.

Good central places with garages for those driving are
**Hostal Pereda** (Valverde 1, tel. 222-4700) and **Hostal Salas**
(Gran Vía 38, tel. 231-9699), £18 ($30) rooms.

We enjoyed the Hotel **Sud-Americana** across from the Prado
Museum (Paseo del Prado 12, 6th floor, tel. 429-2564), £10
($15) doubles, clean, friendly, some traffic noise.

Madrid has two good youth hostels — **Santa Cruz de
Marcenado** (on Calle Santa Cruz de Marcenado 28, tel.
247-4532 near metro stop Arguelles, quite nice in a student
neighbourhood, cheap, 12:30 curfew), and youth hostel **Richard
Schirrman** (Casa de Campo, tel. 463-5699 , near metro El
Lago).

## Food

Madrid loves to eat well. Only Barcelona rivals Madrid in Spain
for eating excitement. You have two basic dining choices: an
atmospheric sit-down meal in a well-chosen restaurant or a
potentially more atmospheric mobile meal doing the popular
'tapa tango' — a local tradition of going from one bar to the next
munching, drinking, and socialising. Dining is not cheap. Tapas
are.

Our favourite sit-down restaurants are: **Zalacaín** (Alvaraz de
Baena 4, closed Sundays and all of August, with garden and
terrace), **El Amparo** (Callejon de Puigcerda 8, closed Sundays
and August), **Jockey** (Amador de los Rios 6 (also closed
Sundays and August). Also good are **Casa Lucio** (Cava Baja 35
in old town), **El Schotis** (Cava Baja 7, closed Sundays and
August), and **Restaurant La Villa de Liuarca** (Concepción
Arenal 6, just off Gran Vía). Restaurants don't get crowded until
after 10:00pm.

Most tourists are drawn to Hemingway's favourite **El Botín**
(Cuchilleros 17 in old town). It's frighteningly touristy. Good
vegetarian food is served at **La Galette** (Conda de Aranda 11,
near Archeological museum). Your hotel receptionist is a reliable

source for more info.

For tapa bars, try this route: from Puerta del Sol head east along Carrera de San Jeronimo, then branch off onto Calles de la Cruz, Echegaray, del Pozo, and Nuñez del Arce.

On Carrera San Jeronimo the atmospheric **Museo del Jamon** ('museum of ham' — note the tasty decor, with smoked ham and sausage lining the ceiling) is a fun, cheap stand-up bar with good bocadillos and raciones.

Each night the Malasaña quarter around the Plaza Dos de Mayo erupts with street life. This is Madrid's new bohemian, intellectual, liberal scene that has flowered only since the death of Franco. Artists, actors, former exiles, and Madrid's youth gather here. **Pepe Botella** is a fun restaurant, and tapa bars abound in this district. Try the old **Café Gijón** (Paseo de Recoletos 21), **Comercial** (Glorieta de Bilbao 10, north of Manuela Malasana) or **Bocaccio.**

After dinner, the best ice cream shops are at Calles Goya 68, Barcalo 1, Tirso de Molina 9, Magallanes 13, Lopez de Hoyos 106.

You'll find live music around Plaza Dos de Mayo and jazz at **Whisky Jazz** (Diego de León 7), **Manuela** (San Vicente Ferrer 29), and **Ragtime** (Ruiz 20). Flamenco is difficult to pin down since the 'in places' change very fast. Try **Arco de Cuchilleros** (Cuchilleros 7, metro stop Sol), **Las Brujas** (Norte 15, metro San Bernardo, tel. 222-5325, 9:30-3am), **Café de Chinitas** (Torija 7), **Cafe de la Moreria** (Moreria 17), or, better still, ask your hotel receptionist.

On this first day in Madrid, you'll have a room by evening, enjoying a relaxing dinner and resting for sightseeing the next day.

## Helpful hints

Madrid's metro — cheap and simple — is the pride of the Spanish public transport system.

Madrid's broad streets can be hot and exhausting. A metro trip of even a stop or two can save time and energy. Once underground, helpful signs show the number of the line and the direction it's heading (eg, '1-Portazgo'). Directions are indicated by end-of-the-line stops. Metros run from 6:00 am to 1:30 am. Pick up a free map ('Plano del Metro') at any station. The Atocha and Chamartin stations are easily reached by metro.

City buses are not so cheap or easy but still good. Get info and schedules at the booth in Puerta del Sol.

Remember, if you're returning to Madrid at the end of your trip, make a reservation at the hotel of your choice. If you pay in advance, you can arrive as late as you like. You can also leave anything you won't need in the hotel's storage room free (have your name and return date clearly indicated). You may also want to reserve a room now for Toledo which can be crowded in July and August.

Because of the threat of terrorist bombs, you can no longer store luggage at the Madrid or Barcelona railway stations. Don't worry though. Local entrepreneurs have set up alternative left luggage facilities just a block or so away.

The main Tourist Information office is at Plaza Mayor 3 (Mon-Fri 10:00-1.30, 4:00-7:00, Sat. 10:00-1:30. tel. 2665477), with other offices on Plaza Espana, in stations and at the airport. Pick up a city map (free) and list of accommodation, confirm your sightseeing plans and hours, and use their handy English language monthly newsletter "En Madrid". "Guîa del Ocio" is another good periodical entertainment guide (available at any kiosk).

The Madrid tourist office can give you info (especially maps) for other Spanish cities you'll be visiting. Pick up what you can; many small town offices keep erratic hours.

# TOUR 2

## MADRID

This is the day for the main sights of Madrid, visiting the Royal Palace and one of the world's greatest art museums, he Prado.

### Suggested Schedule

| | |
|---|---|
| 9:00 | Stroll around Puerta del Sol, through Plaza Mayor and to Palacio Real (Royal Palace). |
| 9:45 | Be at the Palacio Real when it opens. Tour palace, armoury, pharmacy, library. |
| 1:00 | Taxi to the Parque del Retiro. Have a bocadillo (sandwich) in a cafe. |
| 2:00 | Prado Museum. Save time and energy for Picasso's Guernica. (If you're too exhausted by jet lag, do the Prado tomorrow morning). |
| 6:00 | Back to hotel for a rest. Most likely have a simple dinner and surrender to culture shock. |

## Sightseeing highlights

● ● ● **Prado Museum** — Our favourite art museum in Europe. Over 3,000 paintings, including rooms of masterpieces by Velázquez, Goya, El Greco, and Bosch. It's overwhelming. Take a tour or buy a guidebook. See (1) Flemish and Northern art (Bosch, Durer, Rubens); (2) Italian collection (Fra Angelico, Raphael, Botticelli, Titian); and (3) Spanish art (El Greco, Velázquez, Goya).

Follow Goya through his cheery, political ("The Third of May") and dark stages ("Saturn Devouring His Children"). In each of these stages Goya asserted his independence from artistic conventions. Even the standard court portraits of the 'first' stage reflect his politically liberal viewpoint, subtly showing the vanity and stupidity of his subjects by the look in their eyes. His political stage, with paintings like "The Third of May", depicting a massacre of Spaniards by Napoleon's troops, makes him one of the first artists with a social conscience. Finally, in his 'dark stage', Goya probed the inner world of fears and nightmares, anticipating the 20th century preoccupation with dreams. Also, don't miss Bosch's ('El Bosco' in Spanish) "Garden of Earthly Delights".

Good cafeteria, great print and book shop. You can visit twice in one day with the same ticket. Open 10-7, Sunday 10-2, closed

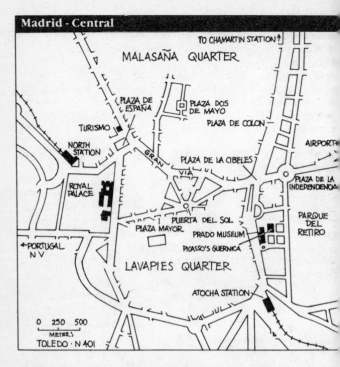

**Madrid - Central**

Mondays. It's free on Saturday, which maximises crowd problems. The quietest time is from 2:00 to 3:00 when everyone breaks for lunch.

● ● **Picasso's Guernica** — In the Casón de Buen Retiro, three blocks east of the Prado. This famous anti-war painting deserves much study. The death of Franco ended the work's American exile and now it reigns as Spain's national piece of art — behind bullet-proof glass. Your Prado ticket is good here, same hours as the Prado except Wednesday, 3-9.

● ● **Royal Palace** (Palacio Real) — Europe's third greatest palace after Versailles and Vienna, and packed with tourists. Lavish interior. English tour included — and required. Open Mon-Sat, 10-12:45, 4-5:45, Sunday 10-12:45.

● ● **El Rastro** — Europe's biggest flea market and a field day for people-watchers. Sunday from 9-2. (There's a smaller version on Fri. and Sat.) Thousands of stalls entertain over a million browsers. If you like car boot sales, you'll love this. You can buy or sell nearly anything here. Start at the Plaza Mayor and head south or take the metro to Tirso de Molina. Hang on to your wallet. Munch on a sweet Pepito or a relleno (sweet pudding-filled pastry). Europe's biggest stamp market thrives simultaneously on the Plaza Mayor.

● ● **Malasaña Quarter** — Night scene and music near the Plaza Dos de Mayo.

● **Chapel San Antonio de la Florida** — The grave of Goya under a cupola filled with Goya frescos. (Mon, Tue, Thur, Sat 10-1, 4-7. Sun 10-1).

● **Retiro Park** — 350 acres of green breezy escape from the city. Hire a boat, have a picnic. Peaceful gardens, great people-watching.

● ● **Bullfight** — Madrid's 'Plaza de Toros' (metro stop: Ventas) hosts Spain's top bullfights nearly every Sunday and many Thursdays from Easter to October. Top fights sell out in advance but you can generally get a ticket at the door. Fights usually start at 7:00 and are one of the few examples of punctuality in Spain. There are no bad seats: paying more gets you in the shade and/or closer to the gore. (Filas 8, 9 and 10 tend to be closest to the action.) Madrid or Seville will probably be your only chances to catch a bullfight in Spain on this tour.

# TOUR 3

## MADRID AND SIDE TRIPS

Today allows you time to soak in some of Madrid's
colourful cosmopolitan atmosphere, return to the Prado, or
take a side trip.

### Suggested Schedule

| | |
|---|---|
| 9:00 | Explore El Rastro flea market (Fri, Sat, or Sun) or just browse through the old quarter south of Puerta del Sol. |
| 11:00 | Chapel San Antonio de la Florida. |
| 1:00 | Afternoon free for side trip, siesta, bullfight (most Sundays, some Thursdays). |
| 8:00 | Stroll around the Malasaña quarter. Find dinner. |

### Side trips from Madrid

**El Escorial** — 30 miles northwest of Madrid. A symbol of power
rather than elegance, this 16th century palace gives us a better
feel for the Inquisition than any other building. Its construction
dominated the Spanish economy for 20 years. For that reason
Madrid has almost nothing else to show from this most powerful
period of Spanish history. This giant gloomy building (grey-black
stone, 2,500 windows, 200 x 150 yards) looks more like a
prison than a palace. 400 years go Philip II ruled his bulky
empire and directed the Inquisition from here. It's full of history,
art and Inquisition ghosts. Open 10-1 and 3:30-6:30, 20 trains a
day from Atocha or Chamartin stations. Upon arrival, get right
on the bus that takes visitors from the station to the palace. By
car: 45 minute drive, out N-VI, turn on C-505.
● ● **La Granja Palace** — This 'Little Versailles' is more enjoyable
than El Escorial. Six miles south of Segovia on N-601, it fits our
plan better as a day trip from Madrid. The palace and gardens
were built by the homesick French king Phillip V, grandson of
Louis XIV. Smaller, more manageable and much less crowded
than its inspiration. Open 10:00-1:30, 3:00-5:00, closed on
Mondays. Fountain displays (which send local crowds into a
frenzy) at 5:30 on Thur, Sat, Sun and holidays. Entry only with
45 minute guided tour (English rare). Wonderful tapestries.
**Avila** — With perfectly preserved medieval walls (to climb them,
enter through the gardens of the *parador*) and several fine
churches and monasteries, this is a popular side trip from

Madrid. Just beyond El Escorial; you could do them together in one day, spending the night in Avila and carrying on to Segovia (4 buses daily) or Salamanca (4 trains daily). Tourist info (9:30-1:30, 4-7) is opposite the cathedral on the main plaza. Pick up a box of the famous local sweets called 'yemas'.

## Itinerary options

If jet lag isn't a problem and there's no flea market or bullfight to hang around for, you may be able to see all you want of Madrid in Tours 1 and 2. This means you could skip Tour 3 using it as a free day to plug in later in your trip. Nearly any longer tour can use a slack day sooner or later. If it turns out you don't need it, enjoy that extra Madrid day at the end of your trip.

Tour 4 is probably the most rushed of our tour. Consider leaving Madrid by noon on Tour 3, checking into a Segovia hotel early and spending the afternoon at La Granja and the evening in Segovia. This leaves Tour 4 and Salamanca much more relaxed. (Again, if you need another day here and aren't into beaches, skip a day at Nazare or the Algarve).

Trains from Madrid: From Madrid's Chamartin station to Barcelona (4 a day, 10-13 hours); to Paris (8 daily, 12-14 hours). From Atocha station to: Lisbon (2 direct trains per day: 10:15-19:05 and 23:30-9:35), Algeciras (2; 12 hours), Cordoba (5; 5-7 hours), Granada (2; 8-10 hours), Segovia (12; 1½-2 hours). From Norte station (Príncipe Pío) to Salamanca (5; 2½ hours).

## TOUR 4

## MADRID — SEGOVIA — SALAMANCA

Today we leave the big city for historic Segovia. Late in
the afternoon we'll carry on to Salamanca to enjoy a
romantic evening on Spain's loveliest town square.

### Suggested Schedule

| | |
|---|---|
| 8:00 | Leave Madrid. |
| 10.00 | Arrive Segovia. Tour Cathedral, Alcazar, Aqueduct. |
| 1:00 | Lunch — roast suckling pig under the Aqueduct. |
| 3:00 | Drive to Salamanca, check in. |
| 6:00 | Tour Cathedrals |
| 8:00 | Dinner and evening on Plaza Mayor. |

### Transport Madrid — Segovia (50 miles)

By car, leave Madrid on Calle Princesa in the direction of Villalba
on N-VI. Turn right onto N-601. The trip takes about 90 minutes,
passing flocks of sheep and going over a 5,000-foot-high
mountain pass.

By bus, leave station La Sepuldevana (Calle Pasco de Florida
11, metro: Norte). There are 4 buses a day (8:00, 11:45, 15:00,
and 19:30) with connections to Avila.

There are 12 trains a day leaving from Atocha station, passing
through Chamartin station.

### Segovia

Just 50 miles from Madrid, Segovia boasts a great Roman
aqueduct, a cathedral, and a castle. It's well worth the better part
of a day. (Elevation 3,000 feet, pop. 55,000, tourist info: Plaza
Mayor 8).

Segovia is a medieval 'ship' ready for your inspection. Start at
the stern — the Aqueduct — then stroll up Calle de Cervantes to
the prickly Gothic masts of the Cathedral. Explore the tangle of
narrow streets around the Plaza Mayor, then descend to the
Alcázar at the bow. To get a quick view of the city's layout, walk
south from the Aqueduct along Avda. de Fernandez Ladredra and
climb the foothills where the city's poor live in shanties with a
beautiful view. The most impressive view of Segovia is one mile
north of town on the road to Valladolid.

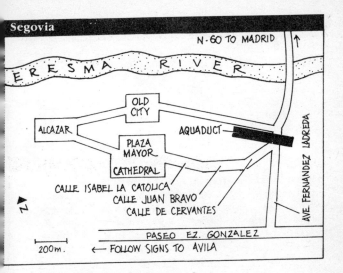

## Sightseeing highlights

● ● **Roman Aqueduct** — Built by the Romans who ruled Spain for over 500 years, this 2,000 year old 'Acueducto Romano' is 2,500 feet long, 100 feet high, has 118 arches, yet was made without any mortar. Climb the stairs at one end to the top of the old city wall where you'll get a good look at the channel that carried the stream of water into the city until the beginning of our century.

● **The Cathedral** — Segovia's cathedral was Spain's last major Gothic building. Embellished to the hilt with pinnacles and flying buttresses, this is a great example of the final 'over-ripe' stage of Gothic called 'Flamboyant'. The spacious and elegant interior provides a delightful contrast. Admission is free (skip the 100 pta. museum), open 10-7.

● **The Alcazar** — This is a Disney-esque exaggeration of the old castle which burned down 100 years ago. Still fun to explore and worthwhile for the view of the cathedral and town from the tower (open 10-7, 125 ptas).

## Accommodation

Look near the Plaza Mayor or the Aqueduct. **Hotel Acueducto** (Av. Padre Claret 10) is a modern-style refuge in this busy area near the Aqueduct, £12 ($20)). The Plaza Mayor is quieter and more central. **Hotel Victoria**, right on the main square, offers surprisingly quiet, basic rooms for £6-9 ($10-15) (Plaza Mayor 5, tel. 435-711). Arrive early in July and August.

## Food

Roast suckling pig (cochinillo asado) is Segovia's culinary claim
to fame and well worth a splurge here (or in Toledo or
Salamanca). The Mesón de Candido (Plaza del Azoguejo 5, near
the aqueduct) is one of the top restaurants in Castile (menu del
dia, £5 ($9)). Also very good is Casa Amado (Ladieda 9). The
best bars and nightlife cluster around Plaza Mayor. Try those on
Calle de Infantes Isabella, especially the very local and busy
Mesón del Campesino (menu del dia, £2 ($3)). Jose Maria
(Cronista Lecea 11) and Tasca la Posada (Judería Vieja 1) are
also good.

## Transport: Segovia — Salamanca (100 miles)

In the afternoon we'll start the easy 2½ drive to Salamanca with
a chance to see Avila en route. Drive south from the Aqueduct
on Avda. Fernandez Ladreda and follow the Avila signs. Just after
the abandoned ghost church at Villacastin turn left on N-501.

When you arrive in Salamanca, park your car and leave it.
Parking is difficult and the town is small enough to manage on
foot. To be safe, park south of the Puente Nuevo (bridge) and
walk into town. If you feel lucky, drive over the bridge, turn right
onto Paseo de Canalejas, then circle the city to the area west of
the Plaza Mayor, turning left at the arrows for 'Centro Ciudad'.

General warning: Leave nothing of value in your car —
especially in large tourist-area car parks. The theft problem
almost vanishes in small untouristed places.

Public transport from Segovia to Salamanca is messy, so if
you're travelling without a car we'd recommend seeing Segovia as
a half day side trip from Madrid and going directly from Madrid
to Salamanca. There are 6 buses a day from Madrid (4½ hours).
The 3½ hour train leaves 4 times a day from Madrid's station
Príncipe Pío, via Avila (8:40, 9:25, 15:40, 19:10). Arriving in
Salamanca, the station is a 15-minute walk from the centre. A
bus will take you to the Plaza Mayor. Train info tel. 212-454.

## Salamanca

Salamanca is Spain's city of grace. Covered with warm
harmonious sandstone architecture, maintaining its university
atmosphere, enjoying its unrivalled main square and thankfully
without the noisy modern sprawl that plagues so many other
cities, this is a great place to spend the night and half a day.

## Sightseeing highlights

● ● Plaza Mayor — 'The' Spanish Plaza, this central square,
built in 1755, is really the best in Spain. A fine place to nurse a
cup of coffee and watch the world go by, and imagine the
excitement of the days when bullfights were held in this square.

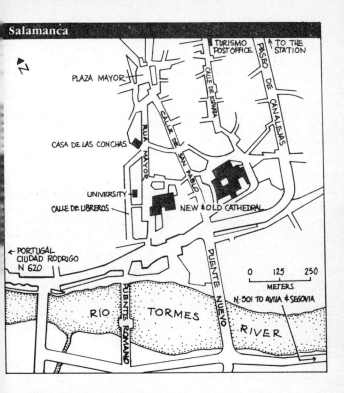

**Salamanca**

● ● **The Cathedral** — Actually two cathedrals — both richly
ornamented — side by side. The 'new' cathedral was begun in
1513 with Renaissance and Baroque parts added later. The old
cathedral goes back to the 12th century. (Open 10-1:45, 4-7:45).

● ● **The University** — Founded in 1230, the Salamanca
University is the oldest in Spain and was one of Europe's finest
centres of learning for 400 years. Columbus came here for help
with his nautical calculations and today many foreigners enjoy its
excellent summer programme. Open Mon-Sat, 9:30-1:30, 4-6.
Explore the old lecture halls where many of Spain's Golden Age
heroes studied. The entrance portal is a great example of Spain's
'Plateresque' style — masonry so intricate it looks like silverwork.

## Salamanca's blood red graffiti

As you walk through the old town or by the cathedrals, you may
see red writing on the walls. For centuries students have
celebrated their PhD graduation by killing and roasting a bull,
having a big feast, and writing their names and new title on a

town wall with the bull's blood. While this is now 'forbidden',
some traditions refuse to die.

## Accommodation
Try to stay near or on the Plaza Mayor. Prices vary from
inexpensive pensiones (**Hostal Los Angeles**, tel. 21-81-66, Plaza
Mayor 10, less than £6 ($10)) to expensive ones (£18-25
($30-40)) with windows right on the square. The **Gran Hotel**
on Plaza Poeta Inglesias 6 (just southeast of Plaza Mayor, tel.
21-3500) offers luxurious doubles for £25 ($45).

## Food
There are plenty of good and inexpensive places between the
Plaza Mayor and the Gran Vía. Try **Las Torres** (Plaza Mayor
26), **Novelty** (Plaza Mayor, great coffee), **Mesón de Cervantes**
(Plaza Mayor, good tapas, sit outside or upstairs), **La
Covachuela** (Plaza Mercado 24), and several places on Calle
Bermejeros (**La Taberna de Pilatos, De La Reina**, and more).
For a special dinner go to **Chez Victor** (Espoz y Mina 22, closed
Sunday and Monday).

For nightlife, be chic at **Gatsby's** in Calle Bordaderos or enjoy
jazz at **El Corillo** just southwest of the plaza.

# TOUR 5

## SALAMANCA – CIUDAD RODRIGO – COIMBRA

After a morning look at Salamanca's university, we'll travel to the old cultural centre of Portugal, Coimbra. En route we'll stop to see a wonderfully preserved and overlooked frontier hill town.

### Suggested Schedule

| | |
|---|---|
| 8:00 | Breakfast on Plaza Mayor, Salamanca. |
| 9:30 | Explore Salamanca University. |
| 10:30 | Drive to Ciudad Rodrigo. |
| 12:00 | Wander around old town and the wall. Lunch. |
| 2:00 | Travel to Coimbra. (Set watch back one hour at border). |
| 6:00 | Explore old town, Coimbra. |
| 8:00 | Dinner. |

### Transport: Salamanca – Ciudad Rodrigo (60 miles)

An easy, boring, but fast drive. There are six buses a day, but from Ciudad Rodrigo the connection to the border is terrible — only one a day. By train, five trains a day go from Salamanca-Ciudad Rodrigo-Fuentes de Onoro-Guarda. Good connections from Guarda to Coimbra and Lisbon.

### Ciudad Rodrigo

This beautiful old town of 16,000 people caps a hill overlooking the Río Agueda. Spend an hour wandering among the Renaissance mansions that line its streets and exploring the 18th century town walls. From these walls you can look into Portugal. The castle is now a luxurious parador (a parador is a government-operated hotel, often a historic castle; all have restaurants). A reasonable way to enjoy this elegance is to splash out for a lunch here. Otherwise head for the Plaza Mayor for a bite to eat. Try coffee and tapas at El Sanatorio (14, Plaza Mayor) or any of the busy bars between the plaza and the cathedral.

Ciudad Rodrigo's cathedral has a special surprise. You'll see a man outside a small door to the cloisters who, for a small price, will take you on a walk through a series of 12th century groin vaults ornamented with stone carvings racy enough to make

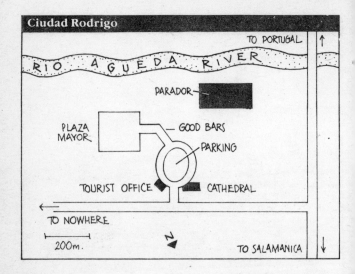

Hugh Hefner blush. Who said "when you've seen one Gothic church you've seen 'em all"?

## Transport: Ciudad Rodrigo — Coimbra (150 miles)

By car the drive is fast, easy, uncrowded and, until Guarda, fairly dull. After Guarda the road winds you through the beautiful Serra da Estrela Mountains. Expect no hassles at the border. Remember, set your watch back one hour as you cross into Portugal. All in all, the drive from Salamanca to Coimbra takes five or six hours. Park the car and leave it (this is an 'on foot' town) along the river on Avda. Emidio Navarro. Leave absolutely *nothing* inside.

There are five trains daily from Ciudad Rodrigo to Coimbra (two are coming direct from Paris, and three require a change in Guarda). The bus station is a mile from the centre down Avda. Fernao Magalhaes. Six or seven buses leave Rodrigo daily to Spain or Lisbon.

## Coimbra — orientation

Coimbra (pronounced KWEEM-bra) is a small town of winding streets set on the side of the hill. The high point is the old university. From there little lanes dribble down to the main business and shopping street, Rua de Ferreira Borges and the Mondego River. The crowded, intense Old Quarter of town is the triangle between the river and the Rua Ferreira Borges. If it's a

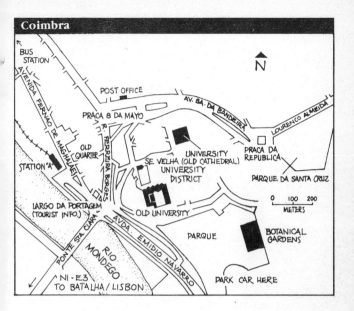

school term, Coimbra bustles. During school holidays, it's more sleepy.

There are two railway stations: A & B. Major trains all stop at B (big). From there it's easy to catch a small train to the very central A station (just 'take the A train'). The tourist info office (Largo da Portagem, tel. 25576, open Mon-Sat 9-8, Sun 10:30-12:30, 2-6) and plenty of good budget rooms are near the A station (train info tel. 34998).

From the Largo da Portagem (main square) everything is within an easy walk. The old town spreads out like an amphitheatre — timeworn houses, shops and stairways, all leading up to the old university.

The most direct route up the hill is to follow Rua Ferreira Borges away from the main square, then turn right under a 12th century arch (the marketplace is down the stairs to your left), up the steep alleyway called Rua de Quebra Costas — 'Street of Broken Ribs'! From the old cathedral, turn right and circle around the old and new university buildings.

## Accommodation

The more comfortable rooms lie on Avenida Emidio Navarro along the river. Try **Hotel Astoria** (at No. 21, tel. 22055, £25 ($40) doubles, rooms facing the hillside are quieter and have a fine city view).

**Pensão Atlantico**, right behind Hotel Astoria, is much more
reasonable (Rua Sargento Mar 42, £8 ($14) doubles). Cheaper
and more interesting places are in the old quarter, especially on
Rua da Sota (leaving Largo da Portagem to the west). There are
plenty of £6 ($10) doubles. Try **Pensão Rivoli** (Praca do
Comercio 27, tel. 25550) or **Residencia Parque** (Avda. Navarro 42,
tel. 29202, river view, English spoken). When all else fails, the 'truck
route' street, Avda. Fernando de Maghalaes, is lined with hotels.

## Food

Most restaurants are near the river. There are a few local-style
cafes near the old cathedral. We enjoyed the stand-up bar **A
Tasquinha** (56 Rua de Quebra Costas). **Restaurant Praca
Velha** (Praca do Comercio 71, on the main square in the
marketplace) is a quiet break from the hectic Old Quarter. A
good place for lunch (cheap, tasty, atmospheric but a bit seedy)
is **Restaurant Alfredo** (cross the bridge, stay to the right, 10
Avda. Joao das Negras).

## TOUR 6

# COIMBRA — BATALHA — NAZARE / SAO MARTINHO DO PORTO

Today we'll tour the historic Coimbra University, then travel to the huge Gothic monastery at Batalha, finally arriving at our beach town headquarters on the Atlantic.

| Suggested Schedule | |
|---|---|
| 8:00 | Breakfast in hotel or with busy locals in a bar on Rua Ferreira Borges. |
| 8:30 | Enjoy a shady morning in the old town alleys and shops. It's about a 15-minute walk to the university. Stop at the old cathedral on your way. |
| 10:00 | Tour the university. |
| 12:00 | Lunch. |
| 1:30 | Drive to Batalha. You'll pass the Roman ruins of Conimbriga and castles at Pombal and Leiria. None of great importance but each interesting if you're interested. |
| 3:30 | Batalha Abbey (Monastery of Sta. María). |
| 5:30 | Drive to São Martinho do Porto. |

## Coimbra

Don't be fooled by the ugly suburbs and monotonous concrete apartment buildings that surround the town. Coimbra was Portugal's most important city for 200 years and second only to Lisbon culturally and historically. It led Portugal while the Moors still controlled Lisbon. Only as Portugal's marine fortunes rose was Coimbra surpassed by the port towns of Lisbon and Porto. Today Coimbra is still Portugal's third largest city (70,000). It has its oldest and most prestigious university (founded 1307) and a great old quarter — with the flavour of a colourful Moroccan Kasbah. The view from the south end of Santa Clara bridge is a great introduction to this town.

## Sightseeing highlights

**Old cathedral (Sé Velha)** — This compact Romanesque building is built like a bulky but dinky fortress, complete with crenellations, with an interesting Flamboyant Gothic altarpiece inside.

● **Old University** — Coimbra's university was modelled after the Bologna University (Europe's first, 1139). It's a stately, three-

winged building located beautifully overlooking the city. At first
Law, Medicine, Grammar and Logic were taught. Then, with
Portugal's seafaring orientation, Astronomy and Geometry were
added. The library has a rich collection of thousands of old
books and historic documents surrounded by gilded ceilings and
baroque halls. The inlaid rosewood reading tables and the shelves
of precious woods are a reminder that Portugal's wealth was
great and it came from far away. Enjoy the panoramic view from
here and imagine being a student in Coimbra 500 years ago.
Don't miss the Manueline-style chapel with its elaborate outside
doors and lavish organ loft. (Open 10-2 and 5-7, ring the
doorbell to get in).

**Old Quarter** — If you can't make it to Morocco, this is the next
best thing for an intense shopping and sightseeing experience.
For a breather, surface on the spacious Praca do Comercio for
coffee or a beer (cerveja).

**Conimbriga Roman Ruins** — Not much of this Roman city has
survived the ravages of time and barbarians. Still, there are
some good floor mosaics and a museum. (7 miles south of
Coimbra on N-1, turn left to Condeixa, open 9-1, 2-8. Museum
closed Mondays).

## Transport: Coimbra — Batalha — São Martinho/Nazare (60 miles)

By car, you'll travel to Batalha on the EN1 (90 minutes). From
Batalha, continuing south on the E1, then veer off following the
signs to Alcobaca on the N8. From Alcobaca you can continue to
Nazare or go straight to São Martinho via Caldas.

The train goes seven times daily from Coimbra to Nazare with a
change in Figueira da Foz. Batalha is reached better by bus. You'll go
to Leiria first (1¾ hours) and catch one of eight daily buses from
there to Alcobaca, via Batalha. From Batalha to São Martinho or
Nazare requires a change in Alcobaca.

São Martinho and Nazare, just 8 miles apart, are connected
by regular buses.

## Batalha — the Monastery of Santa Maria

This is Portugal's greatest architectural achievement and a
symbol of its national pride. Batalha was begun in 1388 to thank
God for a Portuguese victory which kept her free from Spanish
rule. Batalha means 'battle'.

The greatness of Portugal's Age of Discovery shines brightly in
the Royal Cloisters, which manage to combine the sensibility of
Gothic with the elaborate decoration of the fancier Manueline
style, and in the Chapter House with its frighteningly broad
vaults. This heavy ceiling was considered so dangerous to build
(it collapsed twice) that only prisoners condemned to death were

allowed to work on it. Today it's considered stable enough to be the home of the Portuguese tomb of the unknown soldier. Also visit the Founder's Chapel with many royal tombs, including Henry the Navigator's. (Henry's the one wearing a church on his head).

Open 9-7 daily. The Batalha Abbey is great — but nothing else at this stop is. See it, then head on out to the coast.

## Nazare and São Martinho do Porto — Accommodation

Nazare is a fine base town off season, but it's just too crowded in the summer. If you do spend the night, we slept and ate well at the **Pensão-Restaurate Ribamar** Rua Gomes Freire 9, at the west end of the promenade ). Finding a room is almost too easy. You'll be met by plenty of people renting private rooms. Always inspect any room before accepting it.

To avoid the crowds and enjoy a quiet peace of beach, a small village eight miles south is a better stop — São Martinho do Porto ( pronounced 'San Martino' by the not so particular ). There's tourist info right on the beach promenade in the São Martinho town centre. Our favourite accommodation is the **Hotel Parque** ( Av. Marshal Carmona near the post office, tel. 98505, £15 ( $25 ) doubles with stucco ceilings and a peaceful park ). There are several cheaper pensions nearby. The multi-storey hotel behind the Parque is a cheaper modern alternative, full of German holidaymakers ( £13 ( $22 )). Or try the more atmospheric **Pensão Luz** up the hill from the centre of town ( tel. 9-81-39, £7 ( $12 )).

To really escape, go to tiny Salir do Porto nearby. This village has a few private rooms ( quarto ) to rent and virtually no tourism.

## TOUR 7

# SAO MARTINHO / NAZARE – BEACH TIME AND CIRCULAR EXCURSION

After all the travelling you've done, it's time for an easy day and some fun in the sun. Between two nights in our beach town, we'll take a small trip inland, spend the afternoon soaking up the sun, and savour an evening with a large dose of salty fishing village atmosphere.

### Suggested Schedule

| | |
|---|---|
| 8:00 | Breakfast at hotel. |
| 8:30 | Drive through countryside, visiting the wine museum and Alcobaca (town and monastery). |
| 1:00 | Lunch in Nazare, ride funicular up to Sitio, free time on beaches. |
| 7:00 | Seafood dinner — shrimp and vinho verde — watch the boats come in and the sun set. Then return to São Martinho, your quiet base from which to sample other small towns and the nearby resort city of Nazare. |

## Circular excursion through the countryside

Leaving São Martinho ( or Nazare ) you'll drive through eucalyptus groves ( suddenly the world smells like a coughdrop! ) towards Alcobaca, famous for its church, the biggest in Portugal — historic and worth a visit. Alcobaca's market will always shine brightly in my memory. It houses the Old World happily under its huge steel and glass dome. Inside, black-clad, dried-apple-faced women choose fish, chicks, birds, and rabbits from death row. Figs, melons, bushels of grain and nuts — a caveman's Safeway. Buying a picnic is a perfect excuse to take a ride on this magic market carpet.

Just outside town you'll find the local co-operative winery. Its tour, much more 'hands on' than French winery tours, is a walk through mountains of centrifuged, strained and drained grapes — all well on the road to fermentation. The tour climaxes with a climb to the top of one of twenty half-buried 80,000-gallon tanks — all busy fermenting. Look out! I stuck my head into the manhole-sized top vent and just as I focused on the rich bubbling grape stew, I was knocked silly by a wine vapour-punch.

Back in Nazare you'll be greeted by the energetic applause of the forever surf and big plates of smiling steamed shrimp.

## Nazare

In the summer it seems that each of this famous town's 10,000 inhabitants is in the tourist trade. Nazare is a hit with tour groups and masses of Lisbon day-trippers who come up to see traditionally-clad fishermen do everything as traditionally as possible. The beach promenade is a congested tangle of oily sunbathers, hustlers, plastic souvenirs, over-priced restaurants and romantic fishing boats.

Off season, however, Nazare is almost empty of tourists, inexpensive, colourful and relaxed.

Any time of year it's worth a look. Prowl the beach, ride the funicular to the white-washed cliff-top old village of Sitio for the staggering coastal view. Watch out for the traditional outfits the locals still wear. Be on the beach when the fishing boats come in at about 8:00 pm.

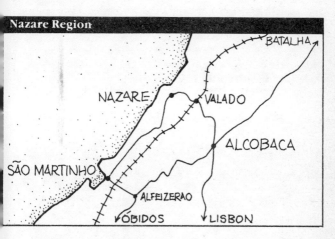

**Nazare Region**

## TOUR 8

# SAO MARTINHO / NAZARE — LISBON

Today we travel about 60 miles, leaving the beach village
to spend a few hours in Portugal's prettiest walled city,
enjoying what is probably Portugal's best seafood for lunch,
and then driving into Lisbon.

### Suggested Schedule

| | |
|---|---|
| 8:00 | Breakfast, drive to Obidos. |
| 9:00 | Explore Obidos. |
| 11:30 | Drive to nearby Ericeira. Lunch. |
| 1:00 | Drive to Lisbon, find your accommodation. |
| 4:00 | Explore Alfama, dinner there. |

### Transport: Nazare / São Martinho — Obidos — Lisbon (60 miles)

Transport becomes more regular as we approach Lisbon. Trains and
buses go almost hourly from Nazare-São Martinho-Obidos-Lisbon.
While Ericeira is served by buses via Torres Vedras and Mafra and
regularly from Lisbon, it's probably worthwhile only if you have a car.

  Both Nazare and São Martinho are on the main Lisbon-Porto
railway line. The Nazare station is three miles out of town near Valado
(easy bus connection) and São Martinho's is about one
mile from town. There are several buses a day from both towns
to Batalha/Coimbra and to Lisbon via Obidos/Torres Vedras.

### Obidos

This medieval walled town was Portugal's 'wedding city' — the
perfect gift for kings to give their queens. Today it is preserved
in its entirety as a national monument, surviving off tourism. You
can drive in, but it's much easier to park outside and walk.

  This postcard town sits atop a hill, its perfect 40-foot high wall
enclosing a bouquet of narrow lanes and flower decked white-
washed houses. Walk around the wall, peek into the castle (now
a lavish pousada — tel. 95105, £25 ($40) doubles), lose yourself
for a while in this lived-in open air museum of medieval city-
planning. It's fun to wander the back lanes, study the solid
centuries-old houses ... and think about progress. There's a small
museum, an interesting Renaissance church with lovely azulejo
walls inside and, outside the walls, an aqueduct and a windmill.

Obidos is crowded in July and August. Filter out the tourists
and it's still great.

Obidos is tough on the budget. The pousada is a wonderful
splurge for lunch. Otherwise pick up a picnic at the grocery shop
near the main gate. If you have time to spend the night you'll
enjoy the town without tourists. The pousada is good value, as is
the Estalagem do Convente, Rua Dr. Joao de Orvelas (tel. 95217,
doubles £12 ($20), just outside the old quarter). For cheap
intimacy ask around for 'quartos', (bed and breakfast). The
Obidos tourist info is open from 9am-8pm. Pick up their handy
town map listing B&B places.

## A Side trip to seafood paradise

Seafood lovers rave about an otherwise uninteresting town called
Ericeira. Just a few miles west from Torres Vedras, this place is a
great lunch stop. Dozens of bars and restaurants pull the finest
lobster, giant crab, mussels and fish out of the sea and serve
them up fresh and cheap. £3 ($5) will buy you a meal fit for
Neptune. Most places are on the main street.

There are good beaches just a few miles north and south of
Ericeira. Buses go several times daily between Lisbon, Sintra and
Ericeira.

## Lisbon — orientation

Lisbon is easy. The city centre is in a valley flanked by two hills.
In the middle of the valley is the Rossio Square, the heart of
Lisbon with plenty of buses, metros and cheap taxis leaving in
all directions. Lisbon's prime attractions are mostly within
walking distance of the Rossio. Between the Rossio and the
harbour is the lower city, Baixa, with its symmetrical street plan,
elegant architecture, bustling shops and many cafes.

On a hill to the west of the Rossio is the old and noble
shopping district of Chiado. Look for shoes, bags, and leather
goods on Rua Garrett and Rua Carmo, and gold and silver on
the Rua do Ouro (Gold Street). Shops are furnished like
museums — don't miss the palatial Grandes Armazenas do
Chiado (Rua do Carmo 2), the Portuguese answer to Harrods.
Above that is the Bairro Alto (upper quarter) with its dark bars,
hidden restaurants, and many *fado* places.

East of the Rossio is another hill blanketed by the medieval
Alfama quarter and capped by the Castelo São Jorge. The
castle offers the best view of Lisbon and a great way to get oriented.
The other great view is from the Bairro Alto on the west hill. Go up
Rua do Misericordia.

Avenida Liberade is the 'Champs Elysées' of Lisbon,
connecting the old lower town with the newer upper end.

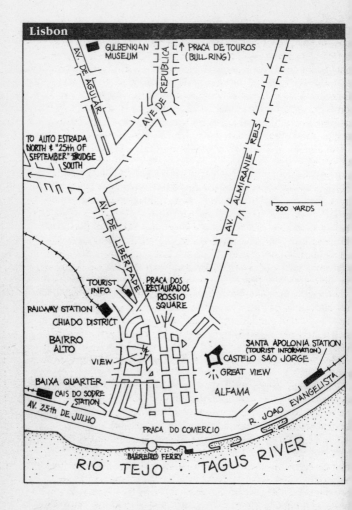

The main Tourist Information office is at the lower end of Ave. Liberdade in the Palacio Foz at Praca dos Restauradores, just north of Rossio (Mon-Sat 9-8, Sun 10-6, tel. 363643; 24-hour telephone service — 893-689). It's friendly and helpful. I even got help pronouncing my basic Portuguese phrases. There are also offices at Castelo São Jorge, in the Apolonia station and at the airport.

Banks, the Post Office, airlines, and travel agents are all along the Ave. Liberdade. In fact, almost any service or information you need can be found in or just off this street.

Lisbon has four stations (see map). Santa Apolonia is the major station, handling all international trains and trains going to north and east Portugal. It's just past the Alfama, with good bus connections to the town centre, tourist info, a room finding service and 24-hour money change service. Barreiro station, 30-minute ferry ride across the Tagus River from Praca do Comercio, is for trains to the Algarve and points south. Rossio station goes to Sintra and the west, and Cais do Sodre station handles the 30-minute services to Cascaís and Estoril.

The airport, just 5 miles northeast of the city centre, has good bus connections to town, cheap taxis, a 24-hour bank and tourist info, and a guarded car park (£1 ($1.50)/day). Tel. 802060.

Lisbon has good public transport. Don't drive your car in the city — park it safely and leave it. Leave nothing valuable in your car and park it in a guarded car park (ask your hotel for advice). The Praca do Comercio at the water's edge has a large car park. This may be your best temporary stop until you locate a hotel.

The Lisbon metro is simple, clean, fast, and cheap, but runs only north of the Rossio into the new town. It runs from 6-1 am. The big letter 'M' marks metro stops.

The bus system is great. Pick up the 'Guia dos Transportes Públicos de Lisboa e Região' for specifics on buses in and around Lisbon. Lisbon's vintage trolley system is as fun and colourful as San Francisco's. Line 28 from Graca to Prazeres offers a great Lisbon joy ride.

Lisbon's taxis are cheap (30p basic charge plus 30p a mile) and abundant.

Thieves abound in Lisbon. Be on a theft alert everywhere, but particularly in the Alfama, Bairro Alto and at night.

## Accommodation

Finding a room in Lisbon is easy. Cheap and charming are on the same see-saw, so the area you choose will generally determine the mix you get. If you arrive late, or in July or August, the room-finding services in the station and at the airport are very helpful. Otherwise, just wander through the district of your choice and find your own bed. If you have a room reserved, take the taxi from the station — it's only 50p or so.

Many pensions (£6-12 ($10-20) doubles) are around the Rossio and in the side streets near the Ave. Liberdade. Quieter and more colourful places are in the Bairro Alto and around the Castelo São Jorge, but those areas are a little on the sleazy side at night.

The **Residencial Nova Silva** (Rua Victor Cordon 11, 2nd floor, 1200 Lisbon, tel. 32-4371 or 32-7770) is a fine budget place with £8 ($14) doubles, views of Tagus River, a little run-down but clean, friendly, English-speaking owner (Mehdi Kara) who will help you phone your next hotel. He'll hold a room if you send a postcard and reconfirm two days in advance by telephone. Has laundry service. Also good is the **Pensão Residencial Campos** on Rua Jardin do Regador 24, 3rd floor, 1100 Lisbon (tel. 32-0560), friendly but no English spoken, very clean and safe, £7 ($12) doubles with showers, no breakfast, lift).

For a bit of extravagance, we've enjoyed the old world **Hotel Borges** (Rua Garrett 108, tel. 361-951, in the Chiado area, £20 ($35) doubles); **Palace Hotel** (grand old atmosphere with crystal chandeliers and heavy furniture, on Rua 1 de Dezembro, tel. 360151, doubles £20-25 ($35-40), in centre between Rossio and Restauradores); **Residencia Caravella** (Rua Ferreira Lapa 38, next to Ave. Duque de Loule, 1100 Lisbon, tel. 539011, comfortable hotel, central, English spoken); and the popular **York House** (also called Residencia Inglesa, pleasant English atmosphere in old villa with garden out toward Belem district at Rua Janeles Verdes 32, tel. 662-435, £18 ($30) doubles).

When searching for a pension, here are some things to remember: singles are a lot more expensive per person than doubles; many buildings have several different pensions, addresses like 26-3° mean number 26, third floor.

To enjoy a more peaceful, old beach resort atmosphere away from the big city intensity, establish headquarters at Cascaís, just 14 miles away. Cheap 30-minute trains go to town several times an hour.

## Food

The smaller pensions actually serve breakfast in bed since they have no dining area. Or try one of the traditional coffeehouses (like the bustling **Cafe Suiza**) on the Rossio.

The best pastry and delicious hot chocolate are at **Ferrari** (Rua Nova do Almada 93). The world's greatest selection of port wines is nearby at **Solar do Vinho do Porto**, on Rua São Pedro de Alcantara 45. For a small price, you can taste any of 250 different ports, though you may want to try only 125 on one night and do the rest the next night.

Lisbon has several great restaurant districts. For lunch (things get going around 12:30) or dinner the Bairro Alto has plenty of small, fun and cheap places. Try the food stalls on the Jardin de São Pedro terrace. The Alfama has many good places along the main street, Rua São Pedro on Largo de São Miguel. For lunch near the Chiado district, try the working man's eating district, Rua Marechal Saldanha, a few blocks west from where Rua Garrett turns into Rua do Loreto (west of Praca do Camoes).

The 'eating lane' — Rua das Portas de Santo Antao — just east of Praca Restauradores, is a galloping gourmet's heaven with all kinds of eateries to choose from. The seafood is great. Rather than siesta, have a small black coffee (called a 'bica') in a shady cafe on the Ave. Liberdade.

Another lunch option is to take a taxi to the Miradouro de Santa Luzia square at the top of the Alfama to the bustling no-name fisherman's hangout just across the street from the square. Shellfish and beer are nearly required here. Castelo São Jorge is just up the hill.

Drop into a few Alfama bars, have an aperitif, taste the blanco seco — the local dry wine. Make a friend, pet a chicken, read the graffiti, study the humanity ground between the cobbles.

For dinner with a great harbour view, try **Faz Figueira** (Rua do Paraíso 15B) or its neighbours in the Alfama. For a simple atmospheric meal (about £2.50 ($4)) try the fishermen's bars on Rua Nova Trinidade in the Bairro Alto. Or back near Praca Restauradores behind Rossio Square consider the restaurant on Rua dos Condotles 29-35 (clean, popular with locals, fresh seafood, good value).

And finally, don't miss a chance to go purely local with hundreds of Portuguese families having salad, chips, chicken and wine at the 'Feira Popular'. More on eating is built into our sample schedules.

# TOUR 9

## LISBON

This is a day for strolling and browsing through Lisbon's tangled jungle of streets and shops.

### Suggested Schedule

| | |
|---|---|
| 8:00 | Breakfast in your hotel. |
| 9:00 | Shopping and browsing in the old Baixa and Chiado quarters. |
| 1:00 | Lunch along Lisbon's 'eating lane' (Rua das Portas de Santo Antāo), or at the top of the Alfama with a view from Castelo Sāo Jorge. |
| 3:00 | Stroll through the Alfama. |
| 8:00 | Dinner, with harbour view. |
| 10:00 | An evening of drink and drone in a Bairro Alto *fado* restaurant (£6-9 ($10-15)). |

### Lisbon

Lisbon is a wonderful mix of now and then. Old wooden trams shiver up and down its hills, bird-stained statues mark grand squares, and people sip coffee in art nouveau cafes.

Present-day Lisbon is explained by its past. While her history goes back to Roman and Moorish days, her glory days were the 15th and 16th centuries when explorers like Vasco da Gama opened up new trade routes making Lisbon Europe's richest city. This economic boom brought the flamboyant art boom called the Manueline period. Later in the early 18th century, the riches of Brazil boosted Lisbon even higher. Then, in 1755, a tremendous earthquake levelled the city killing over 20% of its people.

Lisbon was rebuilt under the energetic leadership of the Marquis Pombal. The grandeur of pre-earthquake Lisbon survives only in Belem, the Alfama and in the Bairro Alto districts. The Pombal-designed centre is on a strict grid plan, symmetrical, with broad boulevards and square squares.

While the earthquake flattened a lot of buildings, and its colonial empire is long gone, Lisbon's heritage is alive and well. Barely elegant outdoor cafes, exciting art, bustling bookshops, entertaining museums, the saltiest sailors' quarter in Europe, and much more, all at bargain basement prices, make Lisbon an Iberian highlight.

## Sightseeing highlights — tour 9

● ● ●**Alfama**—This most colourful sailors' quarter in Europe was the Visigothic birthplace of Lisbon, a rich district during the Arabic period and then the salty home of Lisbon's fisher-folk. One of the few areas to survive the 1755 earthquake, the Alfama is a cobbled cornucopia of Old World colour. Visit during the busy mid-morning market time, or in the late afternoon/early evening when the streets teem with locals.

Wander deep. This urban jungle's roads are squeezed to tangled and confused alleys; bent houses comfort each other in their romantic shabbiness and the air drips with laundry and the smell of clams and raw fish. You'll probably get lost but that doesn't matter — unless you're trying to stay found. Poke aimlessly, sample ample grapes, avoid rabid-looking dogs, peek through windows. This is our favourite European cranny.

'Electrico' trams 10, 11, and 26 go to the Alfama. On Tuesdays and Saturday mornings the 'Feira da Ladra' flea market rages on the Campo de Santa Clara (bus No. 12, tram No. 28).

● **Castelo Sao Jorge** — The city castle with a history going back to Roman days caps the hill above the Alfama and offers the finest view possible of Lisbon. Use this perch to orientate yourself.

● **Fado** — The fado, mournfully beautiful, haunting ballads about lost sailors, broken hearts, and sad romance, is one of Lisbon's favourite late-night pastimes. Be careful, this is also one of those cultural cliches that all too often become tourist traps. The Alfama has many fado bars but most are terribly touristy. The Bairro Alto is your best bet. Things don't start 'til 10:00 and then take an hour or two to warm up. A fado performance isn't cheap (expect £2.50-6.00 ($4-10) cover charge) and many fado joints require dinner. Ask at your hotel for advice. Ja' Disse Restaurant (Rua do Diario 43 in the Bairro Alto) has spontaneous — and therefore sporadic — fado with no cover charge.

## TOUR 10

# THE ART AND HISTORY OF LISBON

After yesterday's plunge into the Lisbon jungle, today we'll concentrate on the 'sights' of Lisbon, the museum and architecture recalling the glory days of Portuguese history.

### Suggested Schedule

| | |
|---|---|
| 8:00 | Breakfast in hotel or in one of the bars on Ave. Liberdade. |
| 9:30 | Catch bus or metro to Gulbenkian Museum. |
| 12:00 | There's a good cafeteria in the museum but we prefer one of Lisbon's best traditional restaurants, the O Policia, just behind the museum on Rua de Sa da Bandeira 162 (closed Sundays). Very popular with locals, unknown to tourists, great seafood meals around 5 ($8). |
| 2:00 | Taxi, bus or tram to Belem to see the glories of Lisbon's golden age. See the Monastery of Jeronimos. Monument to the Discoveries, and Belem Tower for sure. The coach, maritime and pop art museums if you like. |
| 8:00 | Dinner — how about supper in the azulejo-covered cellar of the Bar Trinidade in the Bairro Alto (Rua Trinidade 10). |

## Sightseeing highlights

● **Gulbenkian Museum** — The best of Lisbon's 40 museums. The Armenian oil tycoon, Gulbenkian, gave his art collection (or 'harem' as he called it) to Portugal in gratitude for the hospitable asylum granted him there during WWII. Now this great collection spanning 2,000 years of art is displayed in a classy and comfortable modern building.

Pick up a guidebook in the foyer. Great Egyptian and Greek sections, and a few masterpieces by Rembrandt, Rubens, Renoir, Rodin, and artists whose names start with other letters. Good cafeteria, cheap and air-conditioned, nice gardens. Take bus lines 15, 30, 31, 41, 46, or 56 from the city centre, or Sete-Rios metro line to Palhava stop. Open Tue-Sun 10-5, Wed and Sat until 7 in summer.

● ● ● **Belem District** — The Belem District, 3 miles from the centre is a pincushion of important sights from Portugal's Golden

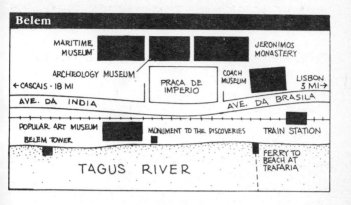

Age, when Vasco da Gama and company made her Europe's richest power. (Bus 12, 29, 43; fun old trams 15, 16, 17 from Praca do Comercio (wave to stop, enter at rear, very cheap, pull tether to ring bell for your stop); or taxi.)

The Belem Tower, the only pure Manueline building in Portugal (built 1515), protected Lisbon's harbour and today symbolises the voyages that made her powerful. This was the last sight sailors saw as they left and the first one they'd see when they returned loaded down with gold, diamonds and spices. (Open Tue-Sun 9-7.)

The giant Monument to the Discoveries was built in 1960 to honour Henry the Navigator who died 500 years earlier. Huge statues of Henry and Portugal's leading explorers line the giant concrete prow.

The Monastery of Jeronimos is possibly Portugal's most exciting building. In the giant church and its cloisters, notice how nicely the Manueline style combines Gothic and Renaissance features with motifs from the sea — the source of the wealth which made this art possible. Don't miss the elegant cloisters — by far my favourite in Europe (open Tue-Sun 10-7).

The Belem museums are somewhere between dull and mediocre depending on on your interests. The coach museum has over 70 carriages from the 18th century. The pop art museum takes you one province at a time through Portugal's folk art. The maritime museum is a cut above the average European maritime museum. Don't miss it if you're a sailor.

**Museum Nacional de Arte Antigua** — Paintings and rich furniture from the days when Portugal owned the world. (Rua das Janeles Verdes 9, open 10-1, 2:30-5. Closed Mondays.)

● **Bullfights** — The Portuguese 'tourada' could be considered a humane version of the Spanish 'corrida' — the Portuguese don't kill the bull. After an equestrian prelude, a colourfully-clad eight-man team enters the ring. The leader prompts the bull to charge and he meets the bull right between the padded horns. As he hangs onto the bull's head, his friends try to wrestle it to the ground. The season lasts from Easter to October and you're most likely to see a fight in Lisbon, Estoril or on the Algarve. Fights start late in the evening. Get schedules at the tourist info.

● ● ●**The Popular Fair** — By all means spend an evening at Lisbon's 'Feira Popular', which rages nightly 'til 1:00 am, May to September. Located on Ave. da Republica at the Entre-Campos metro stop, this fair bustles with Portuguese families at play. Pay the 20 pence entry fee, then enjoy rides, snacks, great people-watching, entertainment, music, basic Portuguese fun. Have dinner here, among chattering families with endless food and wine paraded frantically in every direction. Wine stalls dispense wine from the udders of porcelain cows. Fried ducks drip, barbecues spit and dogs squirt the legs of chairs while, somehow, local lovers ignore everything but each other's eyes.

# TOUR 11

## SIDE TRIPS FROM LISBON

The area to the west of Lisbon is well worth a busy day. A
circular tour, Lisbon — Sintra — Capo da Roca — Cascaís —
Estoril — Lisbon, is a great look at some small but elegant
towns that history has passed by.

### Suggested Schedule

| | |
|---|---|
| 8:00 | Breakfast, travel from Lisbon to Sintra. |
| 9:00 | Sintra, town, Palacio Nacional, Moorish ruins, Pena Palace, Monserrate Park, picnic. |
| 2:00 | Drive to Capo da Roca. |
| 4:00 | Free time in Estoril and Cascaís. |
| 8:00 | Dinner in Cascaís or back in Lisbon. |

### Transport: Circular excursion, Lisbon — Sintra — Capo da Roca — Cascais — Lisbon

This is very easy and most fun by car, and it might be a day
when even bus and train travellers would enjoy a hired car
(several companies on Ave. Liberdade).

Public transport is also good. Trains go from Lisbon to Sintra
(50 min.) and Cascaís (30 min.) three times an hour, and buses
connect points further west. Buses go regularly between Sintra,
Capo da Roca and Cascaís.

### Sintra

Just 12 miles north of Lisbon, this was the summer escape of
Portugal's kings. Byron called it a 'glorious Eden'. It's a lush
playground of castles, palaces, sweeping coastal views and exotic
gardens. You could easily spend a whole day here.

In the town (10 minutes from the station) tour the strange but
lavish Palacio Nacional. Then drive, climb or taxi to the
thousand-year-old Moorish castle ruins. Lost in an enchanted
forest and alive with winds of the past, these ruins are a castle-
lover's dream come true. Great place for a picnic with a
panoramic Atlantic view.

Nearby is the magical hill-capping Pena Palace. Portugal's
German-born Prince Ferdinand hired a German architect to build
him a fantasy castle mixing elements of German and Portuguese
style. He got a crazy fortified salad of Gothic, Arabic, Moorish,
Walt Disney, Renaissance, and Manueline architectural bits and
decorative pieces. The Palace, built in the 1840s, is preserved

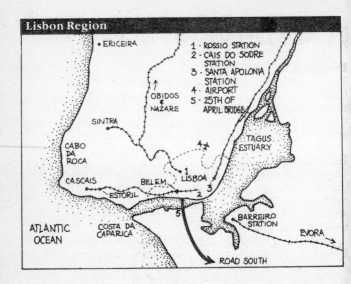

just as it was when the Royal family fled Portugal in 1910. (Open
10-5, closed Tuesdays.)

Also in the area is the wonderful garden of Monserrate. If you
like tropical plants and exotic landscaping, this is definitely for
you.

Nearly everyone who visits Sintra is day tripping from Lisbon.
It's a fine place to spend a night. The **Pensão Nova Sintra** and
**the Estalagem da Raposa** are two of several good — and
nostalgic — hotels. Colares, also near Sintra, is another sleepy place
with a salty breeze. We enjoyed the **Pensão Vareza,** right
in the centre (tel. 299-0008).

## Capo da Roca
The wind-beaten Capo da Roca is the westernmost point in
Europe. This Continental Land's End has a fun little shop and
info booth where you can have a drink and pick up your 'proof of
being here' diploma. Nearby, the Praia (beach) das Macas is a
good place for wind, waves, sand and sun. Buses go regularly
between Capo da Roca, Sintra, and Cascaís.

## Cascaís and Estoril
Before the rise of the Algarve, these towns were the haunt of
Portugal's rich and beautiful. Today, they are quietly elegant with
noble old buildings, beachfront promenades, a bullring and a
casino. Cascaís is the more enjoyable of the two, not as rich and
stuffy, with a cosy touch of fishing village, some great seafood

places (the **Costa Azul**, Rua Sebastio Jose de C. Melo 3) and a younger, less pretentious atmosphere.

## For a swim
The water at Cascaís is filthy, and the city beach at Coasta da Caparica is too crowded. For the best swimming around, catch the bus from Lisbon (3 a day) 30 miles south to the Arrabida Coast. We loved the golden beaches, shellshaped bay, restaurants, and warm clean water at little Port Portinho da Arrabida.

## Itinerary options
Three days in Lisbon is a long time for one stop on this tour. If you need a day to add elsewhere, Tours 9 and 11 could easily be combined (Alfama in the morning, Sintra, Capo da Roca in the afternoon, dinner and evening in Cascaís). You could also skip the Gulbenkian Museum and save half a day.

To save another day, Tour 12 could be snipped by skipping Evora and taking the overnight train direct from Lisbon to the Algarve (or driving there direct via N120, leaving Lisbon at 4:00 and getting to the south coast by 8:00 pm).

# TOUR 12

## LISBON—EVORA—INTERIOR—ALGARVE

Getting from Lisbon to the Algarve can be fast and direct, but that's skipping over a big part of Portugal. Today we'll leave Lisbon early, spend the morning and lunch time in historic Evora, and explore the Portuguese interior's dusty droves of olive groves and scruffy seas of cork trees on our way to the South coast of any sunworshipper's dreams.

### Suggested Schedule

| | |
|---|---|
| 8:00 | Leave Lisbon. |
| 10:00 | Evora sightseeing. |
| 1:00 | Lunch Evora. |
| 2:00 | Drive south. |
| 6:00 | Arrive Lagos. |
| 7:00 | Find private room in Salema on Algarve. |

### Transport: Lisbon — Evora (90 miles)

Drive south over Lisbon's '25th of April' bridge (Europe's biggest suspension bridge, 1½ miles, built in 1966) on the motorway to Setubal and then east (N10, N4, N114) to Evora. The drive should take two hours.

There are five trains a day (2 hours, change at Casa Branca, from Lisbon's Cais do Sodre station) and 10 buses a day (2½ to 3½ hours) that make the trip.

Without a car, consider skipping Evora, going direct from Lisbon to Tavira on the Algarve. Trains and buses go several times a day from Evora to the Algarve but take 6 hours and require a change in Beja. Direct from Lisbon to the Algarve, the train takes 6 hours, a possible overnight trip (Lisbon — Tavira: 8:10-13:55, 9:50-15:41, 14:15-19:32, 22:30-7:00). There are express buses (4-6 hours) that must be booked several hours in advance — get details at the Lisbon tourist office.

Even with a car, Evora is a two-star attraction — and a major detour. It's a pleasant town, rich in history, but consider streamlining your tour by going from Lisbon direct to the south coast. The detour is worthwhile for those seriously interested in Portuguese history and architecture, and who want a look at the old, vast and dusty interior of Portugal.

# Evora

For 2,000 years, Evora has been a cultural oasis in the barren, arid plains of the southern province of Alentejo. With a beautifully untouched provincial atmosphere, a fascinating white-washed old quarter, plenty of museums, a cathedral, and even a Roman temple, Evora stands proud amid groves of cork and olive trees.

The major sights crowd closely together at the town's highest point (Roman temple of Diana, early Gothic cathedral, Archbishop's palace and a luxurious pousada in a former monastery). For osteophiles, see the macabre 'House of Bones' chapel at the Church of St. Francis. It's lined with the bones of 5,000 monks. There's a less tangible but still powerful charm contained within the town's medieval wall. Find it by losing yourself in the quiet lanes of the town's far corners.

The tourist info is at Praca do Giraldo 73 (tel. 22671, open 9-7 daily), and at the city entrance on the road from Lisbon. For budget eating and sleeping look around the central square, Praca do Giraldo. For a spree, sleep in one of Portugal's most luxurious pousadas, the Convento dos Loios (across from the Roman temple, tel. 23079, £20 ($35) doubles). The best food we found is at **O Fialho** (at Travessa Mascarhenas 14, phone 23079 to make a reservation, £6 ($10) meals). For very local atmosphere eat at the **Restaurant** restaurant just off the Praca at 11 Rua Romão Romalha.

## Transport: Evora — Lagos / Salema on the Algarve (150 miles)

After lunch head south, exploring the plains and small towns of the dusty and depressed part of Portugal. From Evora, drive south to Beja, west to Aljustrel, then south by any number of equal routes. The fastest is to follow the signs southwest to Odemira, then turn south toward Albufeira. All the roads are a mix of straight and winding, smooth and washboard, and you'll spend your share of time in third gear. The main N120 road is slow and crowded. The Lisbon-Lagos highway is excellent. Expect good roads but more traffic in the Algarve.

Train service from Lisbon to the Algarve (6 hours, four or five a day, overnight journey possible) is pretty good, and it's excellent between major towns along the south coast (nearly hourly between Lagos and the Spanish border). Buses will take you where the trains don't.

## The interior

The villages you'll pass through in southern Alentejo are poor, quiet and, in many cases, dying. Unemployment here is so bad that many locals have left their hometowns for jobs — or hope of jobs — in the big city. This is the land of the 'black widows' —

women whose husbands have abandoned them to get work in the cities.

Beja, with its NATO base, is nothing special. Its castle has a military museum and a territorial view (open 10-1, 2-6), and the old town is worth a look and a cup of coffee.

A more enjoyable stop on your drive south would be for a refreshing swim in one of the lonely lakes of the Alentejo desert — for example, Baragem do Maranho or Baragem do Montargil.

Plan on arriving at the resort town of Lagos on the southern coast by 6:00. From here drive west about halfway to Cape Sagres, then turn south down the small road to the small beach town of Salema.

## Salema — accommodation and food

Skip the hotels and ask in the bar, at the post office or on the beach for 'quarto' (bed and breakfast). Along the road running left from the village centre as you face the beach, you'll find plenty of friendly locals with 'Rooms to Let £2.50 ($4.50)'. Most houses have decent plumbing and many rooms have a beach-front balcony or view. Try the white two-storey **Bar Carioca** (with the parrot painted on the side) 30 yards off the beach for the hip hangout. Or for a more peaceful room, knock on the little green door across the street from the mini-market. Few of the locals speak English but that isn't a problem. Campers do fine just sleeping on the beach (free showers nearby), or they can enjoy the fine new campsite just half a mile inland back toward the main road.

I had my breakfast and dinners at the beachfront restaurant where the town's visitors gather each night. Their octopus salad will really grab you. (Or it may 'greet you with open arms').

## Option: Tavira

Those without a car will find Tavira easier to manage than Salema with a direct Lisbon train connection, easier trip to Seville, a still good — if not so small-town — Algarve atmosphere, ten-minute walk from station to town centre. A five-minute ferry ride connects town with a fun little beach island. Sleep at **Lagoas Bica**, Rua Almirante Candido dos Reis 24, 8800 Tavira, tel. 22252. This residencia is clean, friendly, speaks some English, communal refrigerator, rooftop patio, courtyard garden; £7 ($12) doubles with shower. The riverfront **Restaurante Beira Rio** on Rua da Borda de Agua Asseca serves a fine dinner — tuna and shark.

# TOUR 13

## SALEMA, YOUR ALGARVE HIDEAWAY

Today will be a day of rigorous rest and relaxation on the beaches of Salema and in town.

### Suggested Schedule

| | |
|---|---|
| 9:00 | Breakfast and relax on the beach. |
| 12:00 | Lunch and relax on the beach. |
| 1:00 | Relax on the beach, browse around town. |
| 6:00 | Keep on relaxing. |

### The Algarve

The Algarve, Portugal's southern coast, has long been known as Europe's last undiscovered frontier'. That statement, like 'military intelligence' and 'jumbo shrimp', contradicts itself. The Algarve is well discovered and most of it is going the way of the Spanish Costa del Sol: paved, packed and stressful.

One bit of old Algarve magic still glitters quietly in the sun — Salema. At the end of a small road just off the main road between the big city of Lagos and Europe's rugged 'Land's End', Cape Sagres. This fishing village, quietly discovered by British and German tourists, is the best beach town left on the Algarve. It has a few hotels, time-share apartments up the road, some 'hippies', bars with rock music, English and German menus and signs (bullfight ads for 'stierskampf'), but it's not a resort. Lovely beach and lots of sun. From June to September buses connect Lagos and Salema (5 a day, under 1 hour).

### Algarve Coast

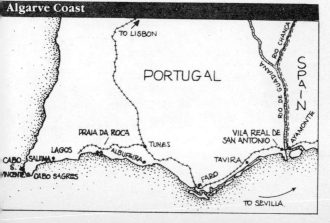

# TOUR 14

## SIDE TRIP TO SAGRES

A short trip in the morning to Cape Sagres, then more free time in Salema and Lagos. It's a tough life.

### Suggested Schedule

| | |
|---|---|
| 8:00 | Drive to Cape Sagres. |
| 8:30 | Breakfast at Pousada do Infante. |
| 9:30 | Explore the cape, the fort and the rugged nearby Cabo de São Vicente. |
| 12:30 | Picnic lunch on beach at Beliche. |
| 1:00 | Siesta on beach and free afternoon. Options: explore the west coast (Carrapateira is a lovely town), have a look at the nearest big city resort, Lagos, and the famous Praia da Rocha near Portimao. This beach is the focal point of Algarve tourism. Or, go back to Salema and see how slow you can get your pulse. |
| 8:00 | Dinner in Lagos if you want some action, or in Salema if a sunset and fresh fish are enough of a thrill. |

### Cape Sagres

From Salema it's a short drive or hitch to the rugged and historic southwest tip of Portugal. This was the spot closest to the edge of our flat earth in the days before Columbus. Prince Henry the Navigator, who was determined to broaden Europe's horizons, sent sailors even farther into the unknown. He had a special navigator's school at Cape Sagres. Henry carefully debriefed the many shipwrecked and frustrated explorers who washed ashore here.

Today fishermen cast from its towering crags, local merchants sell seaworthy sweaters, and the windswept landscape harbours sleepy beaches, a salty village and the lavish **Pousada do Infante**. For a touch of local elegance, drop in at the pousada for breakfast.

# TOUR 15

# THE DRIVE TO SEVILLE

After several days of storing up solar energy, it's time to hit the road again to return to Spain, spending the night in Seville.

## Suggested Schedule

| | |
|---|---|
| 8:00 | Breakfast and hit the road, driving east toward Spain. |
| 10:00 | Coffee break and a wander through the super touristy but still nice resort town of Albufeira. |
| 11:00 | Drive further east. |
| 1:00 | Lunch in Tavira. |
| 3:30 | Catch ferry in Vila Real to Spain. Set watch ahead one hour.) |
| 6:00 | Arrive in Seville. |

## Transport: Algarve — Seville (150 miles)

Drive east along the Algarve. (If the traffic is bad take the smaller N270 road to Tavira. It's about a 2½ hour drive from Salema to Tavira.) At Vila Real you'll catch the inexpensive 5-minute ferry across the river to Spain. It leaves every thirty minutes from 8 am to 10 pm, May-October, and 8 am to 7 pm in the off season. Despite the frequency of ferries, cars can queue for several hours. (Note: the ferry isn't always loaded in an orderly first-come first-served manner. So if you see a queue of cars moving, get in it.) Once across the river to Ayamonte, there's a great road straight into Seville (50 miles).

The town of Vila Real has plenty of rooms, good people watching, and Saturday night bullfights but is nothing special. Nearby Tavira is a better place if you want one last night in Portugal.

Buses and trains go almost hourly connecting most towns along the south coast from Sagres to Vila Real, where you catch the ferry to Ayamonte, Spain. Vila Real has two stops: central and the ferry dock. Take the second stop. From Ayamonte, the Spanish border town, catch a bus or train. By bus it's a pain. Three a day (10, 2, and 6:00) to Huelva where a train takes you to Seville. The railway station is a 25-minute walk from the ferry — take a taxi. Trains leave from Ayamonte at 7:00, 11:00 and 16:00. Don't miss the 11:00 Seville train. Consider hitching a ride from the ferry traffic instead. Remember, you lose an hour when you cross into Spain, so set your watch ahead.

## Seville — orientation

For the tourist, this large city is small. Think of things relative to the river and the cathedral — which is as central as you can get. The major sights surround the cathedral. The central boulevard, Ave. de la Constitución (tourist info, banks, post office, etc) zips right by the cathedral to the Plaza Nueva (shopping district), and nearly everything is within easy walking distance. Pick up the excellent map/brochure at the tourist office.

By car, follow signs to 'centro ciudad'. During July and August don't park on Paseo de Cristobal Colón ('Columbus' in Spanish) Seville is Spain's capital of splintered windscreens. There is a guarded underground garage where you can leave your car safely.

## Accommodation

Seville has plenty of £5-12 ($8-20) doubles. The best areas are in the triangle between the Cordoba station, the bull ring, and the Plaza Nueva and in the Santa Cruz district (lots of hostales and fondas. traffic-free, great atmosphere). There are many budget hotels along the Calle Zaragoza a few blocks off the Plaza Nueva; the farther from the Plaza, the cheaper they get. Our favourite budget bet is the **Hostal Goya** (Mateos Gago 31, tel.

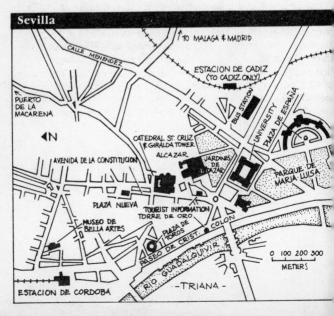

Sevilla

211170), two minutes from the back of the cathedral, £15 ($25)
doubles, nice courtyard. For luxury complete with antiques, old
paintings, and four-poster beds, try the **Hotel Doña Maria** (Don
Remondo 19, Seville 4, tel. (954) 22-4990, quiet street next to
cathedral, £25 ($40) doubles, great value) or **Hostal Monreal**
in Barrio Sta. Cruz, (Calle Rodrigo Caro 8 tel. 213166, about £7
$12) for a double). Two minutes from the railway station is
**Hostal Residencia Arizona** (Pedro del Toro 14, tel. 216042),
£6 ($10) doubles, clean, decent, safe but traffic noise and
sagging double beds.

## Food

For tapas there are several good bar-hopping areas: 1) Barrio
Sta. Cruz — especially the Bodega right on Mateos Gago, two
blocks from the Cathedral. Try **Lucas' Bar**, a hole in the wall
(actually 8 Doncellas) near the Plaza Sta. Cruz. His sketches
cover the walls and he's an artist behind the bar as well. 2)
Triana district — on the other side of the river. Up-market bars
line the river, workingmen's places are one block in. **La Taberna**
(half-block back, between the two bridges, next to police station)
is cheap, youthful, and lively after 11:00 pm. 3) The area one
block west of Avda. de la Constitución.

For a non-tapas lunch there are plenty of places in the
Cathedral/Santa Cruz area — touristy, but reasonable.

For dinner, if you're tired of tapas, you can splash out at the
**Rio Grande** restaurant (across the river, shady deck over the
river, good view, good food and good service, £6-9 ($10-15) or
eat the same thing next door at the self-service **El Puerto** for a
third of the price. In the Barrio Sta. Cruz, **La Posada** serves
fine inexpensive meals in wonderful atmosphere — outdoors, view
of Giralda, swallows and bats circling above. In Seville, dinner
starts no earlier than 8:30.

# TOUR 16

## SEVILLE

'Seville doesn't have ambiance, it *is* ambiance.'
— *James A. Michener*

### Suggested Schedule

| | |
|---|---|
| 8:00 | Breakfast — probably in hotel. If not, go in small bars between Paseo de Cristobal Colón and cathedral. |
| 9:00 | Alcazar and garden — beat the crowds, silent beauty. |
| 11:00 | Cathedral and Giralda tower. After a cafe con leche across from the cathedral, tour this giant church. Climb the tower. What a view! |
| 1:00 | Barrio de Santa Cruz. Stroll through the old Jewish Quarter, peek into private patios, feel the atmosphere. |
| 1:30 | Lunch. Head for the river. Too much to eat? Sleep it off in the shady Maria Luisa Park. It's siesta anyway and nothing's happening until 3:00 or 3:30. |
| 3:30 | Shopping. Get things rolling again. Taxi to the Plaza Nueva, have a cafe con leche and just stroll. |
| 5:00 | La Macarena. Take a cab to the Weeping Virgin. Explore behind the altar. |
| Evening | Relax at the hotel, take a stroll through the Barrio de Santa Cruz and up toward the Plaza Nueva for a nightly people parade. By then it's time to dine. Flamenco is best around midnight. |

## Seville

This is the city of flamenco, Carmen, Don Giovanni, and, of course the Barber of Seville. While Granada has the great Alhambra, Seville has a soul — one of south Spain's most pleasant cities.

Seville boomed when Spain did. She was the gateway to the New World. Explorers like Amerigo Vespucci and Magellan sailed from her great river habour. Seville's Golden Age with New World riches and great local artists (Velázquez, Murillo, Zurbaran) ended with the silting up of the harbour and the crumbling of the Spanish Empire.

Today Seville (pop. 680,000) is Spain's fourth largest city and Andalucia's number one city. She buzzes with festivals, life, and colour.

# Sightseeing highlights

● ● **Cathedral** — The third largest church in Europe (after St. Peter's and St. Paul's) was built that way on purpose. When the Catholics ripped down a mosque on the site in 1401 they said, 'Let us build a cathedral so huge that anyone who sees it will take us for madmen'. Though no longer the largest, it remains among the ugliest, in a fascinating way. Very late Gothic style with some Renaissance. Don't miss the Royal Chapel, Sanctuary, the grotesque Head of John the Baptist statue in the Reliquary which has absolutely no historic or artistic significance) and Columbus' tomb. Open 10:30-1, 4:30-6:30.

● **Giralda Tower** — Formerly a Moorish minaret used to call the Muslims to prayer, it became the cathedral's bell tower after the Reconquista. Notice the beautiful Moorish simplicity as you climb to its top, 100 yards up, for a grand city view. Take advantage of this bird's eye perspective to orientate yourself. Open same hours as cathedral.

● ● **Alcazar** — Much of this Moorish palace was rebuilt by the Christians. The Alcazar is an impressive collection of royal courts, halls, patios, and apartments. The garden is full of tropical flowers, wild cats, cool fountains, and hot tourists. Try to enjoy this peace at 9:00 am. Open 9-12:45, 3-5:45, closed Sundays.

● ● **Barrio de Santa Cruz (the old Jewish quarter)** — Even if it is a little over-restored, this classy world of lanes too narrow for cars, whitewashed houses with wrought-iron lattice work, and azulejo-covered patios is a great refuge from the summer heat and bustle of Seville. Plenty of tourist shops, small hotels, and flamenco bars.

**University** — Today's university was yesterday's 'Fábrica de Tabacos' which employed 10,000 young female cigareras — including Bizet's 'Carmen'. The university's bustling cafe is a great place for cheap tapas, beer, wine and conversation. The second largest building in Spain, after the Escorial. Plenty of student bars and atmosphere between here and the river.

**Belas Artes Museum** — Seville's top collection of art, with 50 Murillos and some Velázquez paintings.

● **La Macarena Virgin** — This altarpiece statue of the Weeping Virgin — complete with diamond teardrops — leads Seville's grand processions. She's so beautiful in her special chapel just off the

Puerta Macarena. Take a taxi. Open 9:30-1, 5-8.
**Bullfights** — The most artistic and tradition-bound bullfighting in
Spain is done in Seville. Most Sundays in the summer.
**Plaza de España** — Lovely square, historical blue and white tiles,
people watching, and a great park — Maria Luisa — nearby.
**April Feria** — Seville's famous five-day fiesta (usually two weeks
after Easter) is exciting, colourful, and very very crowded. Plenty
of traditional costumes, flamenco dancing and daily bullfights.
● ● ● **Evenings** — Seville is a town meant for strolling. The area
around the Plaza Nueva thrives throughout the evening. For a
competent but touristy flamenco show, your hotel can get you
tickets for about £7 ($12). ('La Trocha', Ronda de Capuchinos 23,
tel. 355028, 9 pm-2 am; 'Los Gallos', Plaza de Santa Cruz 11, tel.
216981, 9:30-11:30 pm and 11:30-2 am.) However, the best
flamenco erupts spontaneously in bars throughout the old town.
Just follow your ears in the Barrio de Santa Cruz. Try 'La
Carboneria' (Levies 18, near Hotel Fernando III), a former
charcoal factory and now a bohemian hangout with a pleasant
courtyard. Flamenco rarely rolls before midnight.
**Italica** — Excursion for ruins fans. Roman site from 200 B.C., six
miles by bus near Santiponce. Third largest Roman amphitheatre

# TOUR 17

## SEVILLE — ANDALUCIAN VILLAGES — RONDA

Today is small Andalucian town day. We'll leave Seville early, arrive in Ronda late and get the best look possible at southern Spain's 'Ruta de Peublos Blancos' — the route of the white villages.

### Suggested Schedule

> Armed with a good map, hit the back roads and explore.
> Spend the night in a small town, possibly Estepa or the larger Ronda.

Obviously this Andalucian wander day could easily stretch to two or three days. The best towns fall roughly within a triangle formed by Granada, Seville and Ronda.

By car you'll hit a good sampling of villages. By bus it'll be slower going, and the schedules rather than your whim will dictate your plans. If you're considering hitchhiking, think of hiring a mule instead — it's faster.

Since these towns have very little tourism, accommodation is rather scarce. Still, a night in a small town is a wonderful experience.

### Transport

This day is really designed for those with a car. The roads are good, the traffic is light. Car hire is inexpensive, and public transport is sparse. Pick up the 'Ruta de Pueblos Blancos' brochure from the Seville tourist info, get a good map, hit the back roads and find that perfect village.

The Seville-Ronda train connection is miserable, but there are four direct buses a day (5 hours). The bus station, serving Portugal and Andalucia, is a 5-minute walk from the Alcazar in Plaza de San Sebastian.

Other train connections from Seville's Cordoba station are very good. From the Cordoba station: to Madrid (four a day, 8-10 hours); to Cordoba (two a day, 4½ hours); to Málaga (two a day, 3½ hours). There is a 'directo' to Granada, 7:20-12:10 — consider this if you need to streamline your trip, and skip the beaches and Andalucian towns. As in several Spanish stations, there may be no luggage lockers available because of bomb threats.

## Andalucia

Half the towns I visited were worth remembering. Noteworthy towns are easy to find so don't worry about missing our favourites. Good information on Andalucia is as rare as it is important — very. There just isn't much written on the interior. The Michelin guide skips it. Get the best map you can find (Michelin No. 446), look for locally printed books as you're travelling and ask the people you meet for touring suggestions. Some tourist offices have a handy 'Ruta de Pueblos Blancos' brochure. Here are a few ideas for starters:

## Some favourite hill towns

Our favourite Andalucian discovery is **Estepa**. Except for the busy truck route that skirts the town, peace abounds. Estepa hugs a small hill halfway between Cordoba and Málaga. Its crown is the convent of Santa Clara, worth five stars in any guidebook but found in none. Enjoy the territorial view from the summit, then step into the quiet spiritual perfection of this little-known convent. Just sit in the chapel all alone and feel the beauty soak through your body.

Evening is the best time in Estepa — or any Andalucian town. The promenade; or 'paseo', begins as everyone gravitates to the central square. Estepa's spotless streets are shined nightly by the feet of ice cream-licking strollers. The whole town strolls — it's the 'done thing'. Buy an 'ice cream bocadillo' and follow suit. There's a great barber — a real artist — located right on the square. Good chance to make a friend and get a trim. (Driving: Seville-Estepa, 2½ hours on N334. Estepa to Ronda, 2 hours on N334, N342 to Campillos, and C341 into Ronda.)

**Ortegicar** — This is a teeny 6-horse, 10-dog complex of buildings around a castle keep. (½ mile off C341 on a dirt road. 7 miles north of Cuevas del Becerro on the way to Ronda.)

South of Estepa is hill-capping **Teba**, where the people go into hysterics when you take their picture. **Menzanares** and **Carratraca** are also stop-worthy. The Michelin guide raves about the Chorro Gorge. Skip it — it's not worth the drive unless you're a real gorge-ophile.

To the north, **Aguilar de la Frontera** and **Puente-Genil** are nice. Aguilar has a pleasant square, outdoor dancing and people who are fascinated by tourists with hairy legs.

A great motorway connects Seville and **Jerez de la Frontera**. Jerez, with nearly 200,000 people, is your typical big city mix of industry, rubbish and dusty concrete suburbs, but it has one popular claim to tourist fame — it's the home of sherry. If you're interested, stop at the **Bodega of Pedro Domeca** (Calle San Ildefonso 3, outside town on the road to Cadiz, tel. 331900, open Mon-Sat 9:30-12:30, closed July). He's the world's biggest

**Costa Del Sol**

producer of sherry and brandy. A free guided tour will show you the whole enchilada including a look at the oldest sherry in the world, 240 years old. After the one-hour tour you're rewarded with several samples to taste.

To return to the pretty little towns of this region, drive to **Arcos de la Frontera** (de la Frontera refers to frontier towns from the days when the Christians were pushing the Moors south). Arcos is spectacularly situated on a pinnacle overlooking a vast Andalucian plain. Climb to the church's bell tower — through the tower-keeper's home — for the best view and an ear-shattering thrill at the top of the hour. Driving in Arcos is like threading needles with your car. The Casa del Corregidor parador here is great (tel. 700460).

Just past Arcos on the road to Ronda (the C344) is a reservoir in a pine forest with a great beach. A swim here is refreshing, and if you decide to extend your siesta, you'll find a hotel and a good eating place, Meson del Brigadier.

Take the lonely, quiet and beautiful small road from Arcos to Ronda via El Bosque. Over a pass you'll come to **Grazalema**, another postcard-pretty white town and a fine base for a hike in the Sierra de Grazalema.

Near Ronda are two more white wonders — **Zahara**, with a couple of good budget pensions, and the curiously situated **Setenil**.

As you explore Andalucia on a hot summer day you may see a curious natural phenomenon — the Calina. As the warm air rises, it lifts dust from the bone dry ground. On a windless day, this dust puddle paints the landscape a rusty brown as villages grow hazy and fade into the horizon. The Calina is most common near Ubeda around the headwaters of the Guadalquivir.

## Ronda

Ronda is the capital of the 'white towns'. With 40,000 people it's one of the largest, and since it's within easy day trip range of the 'Costa del Turismo', it's very crowded. Still, it has the charm, history and bus and train connections to make it a good stop.

Ronda's main attractions are the gorge it straddles, the oldest bullring in Spain and an interesting old town.

## Orientation

Ronda's breathtaking ravine divides the town's labyrinthine Roman/Moorish quarter and its new, more noisy and sprawling Mercadillo quarter. A graceful 18th century bridge connects the two halves. Most things of tourist importance cluster within a few blocks of this bridge — the sights, bullring, view, tourist info, post office and hotels.

The train and bus stations are 15 minutes by foot from the bridge in the new town. The tourist office is on the square next to the bridge. (Open Mon-Fri 9:30-2, 5-7, Sat 9:30-2, tel. 871272.)

## Accommodation

Places in the Old Quarter are overpriced. There are plenty of inexpensive places (£6 ($10)) in the new town, especially along Calle Sevilla and near the Plaza de España. Try **La Española Huespedes** just off the Plaza de Espana in the alleyway behind the tourist info office. Choose a place with street noise in mind. The best 'spend' is the royal **Reina Victoria** (24 Jerez, tel. 871240) hanging over the gorge at the edge of the town. It's a great view — Hemingway loved it — but you'll pay for it (£30 ($50) doubles). Our favourite £20 ($30) room is at the **Hotel Residencia Polo** (8 Padre Mariano Soubiron, tel. 87-24-47).

## Food

Try to avoid the tourist traps. One block from the bullring is the Plaza del Socorro with plenty of cheap tapa bars and restaurants. **Las**

**Canas** at 2 Duque de la Victoria on the corner of the plaza is small, simple, and serves great food.

## Side trip — Pileta Caves

The 'Cuevas de la Pileta' are about the best look a tourist can get at prehistoric cave painting. The cave, complete with stalagmites, bones and 25,000-year-old paintings, is 17 miles from Ronda. By car it's an interesting drive: go north on C-339, exit toward Benoajan, then follow the signs, bearing right just before Benoajan, up to the dramatic deadend. Or take the train to Benoajan and walk in (90 minutes).

The farmer who lives down the hill leads groups through from 9 to 2 and from 4 to 7. (His grandfather discovered the caves.) If he's not there, the sign says to yell for him. He is a master at hurdling the language barrier, and as you walk the cool kilometre he'll spend an hour pointing out lots of black and red drawings (five times as old as the Egyptian pyramids) and some weirdly recognisable natural formations. . .like the Michelin man and a Christmas tree. The famous caves at Altamira are closed, so if you want to see Neolithic paintings, this is a must.

# TOUR 18

## RONDA TO THE COSTA DEL SOL

After a morning stroll through Ronda, we'll make the 40-mile journey from the serenely sublime to the raucously ridiculous: from the untouristed, whitewashed towns of Andalucia to the hypertouristed, concrete-paved resorts of the exciting Costa del Sol. Don't think of it as a holiday, but an experiment in sociology.

### Suggested Schedule

| | |
|---|---|
| 8:00 | Breakfast. |
| 8:30 | Explore Old Ronda, the gorge and bullring. |
| 11:30 | Drive 40 miles to the Costa del Sol. |
| 1:00 | Lunch and afternoon in resort of your choice: Marbella/Puerto Banus — home of the rich and beautiful; Fuengirola — the package tourist's Mecca; Nerja — quiet and intimate, by resort standards. |
| 6:00 | Experience the tacky but fun Costa del Sol resort scene. |

## Sightseeing highlights — Ronda

● ● **Old Quarter** — East of the bridge, this natural fortress-town has kept much of its Roman Moorish and Renaissance flavour. Don't miss the Casa del Rey Moro ('House of the Moorish King') built in the 18th century on Moorish foundations. From its garden, you can walk down an underground stairway — 365 steps to the river below — cut by Christian slaves in the 1300s. Next door you'll see four funny 'savages' carved in the doorway.

● ● **Puente Nuevo** and **The Guadalevin River Gorge** — Enjoy the view from the bridge, especially at sunset, and the hike into the gorge.

● **Plaza de Toros** — One of the oldest bullrings in Spain (1785). Ronda is known as the birthplace of modern bullfighting. It's also the home of Pedro Romero, one of Spain's greatest early matadors (open 9-7).

**The 'Corrida Goyesca'** — A great feria held in early September with plenty of bullfighting, flamenco dancing, traditional costumes, and crowds. (Tickets are tight. Make reservations after Aug 30 at Toros de Ronda, tel. 925-872529.)

**Best views:** Puente Nuevo, Alameda del Tejo Park, Hotel Reina

Victoria (just walk through the lobby as if you're there to meet
Hemingway).

## Transport: Ronda — Costa del Sol (40 miles)

By car this can be fast and direct or, if you've yet to quench
your hilltown thirst, take the longer but very scenic southern
route via Gaucín, Jimena and Castellar. The quickest route to the
coast is through the old town and south on the C-339. There are
four daily 4-hour bus services from Ronda to Málaga, and many
others that make stops all along the Costa del Sol. With no car,
if you're short on time, consider skipping the Costa del Sol and
going by train straight to Granada.

Along the Costa del Sol, it's smooth and easy by car (great
roads across the whole region) and more frustrating by bus or
train. The super-developed area between Málaga and Fuengirola
is well served by trains (twice an hour, 43 minutes from Málaga
to Fuengirola) and buses.

The tiny village of Bobadilla is the unlikely hub of Spain's
southern train system. Train travellers, never by choice, always
have more than enough time to get to know 'Bob'. Here are the
basic departure times you may be dealing with:

**Bobadilla to Málaga:** 40 miles, l hour (dep. 10:30, 12:29,
15:15, 20:14).
**Bobadilla to Granada:** 70 miles, 2 hours ( 10:36, 15:20, 20:01 ).
**Bobadilla to Ronda:** 40 miles, 80 minutes ( 10:41, 11:20, 15:35,
17:13).
**Bobadilla to Seville:** 100 miles, 2½ hours ( 15:23, 19:58).
**Seville to Bobadilla:** 2½ hours (8:05, 12:00, 17:25).
**Ronda to Bobadilla:** 1¼ hours (8:53, 10:10, 13:35, 18:16,
23:54).

The trip from Bobadilla to Málaga via El Choro is one of
Spain's most scenic mountain routes.

## Costa del Sol

The Costa del Sol is so bad it's interesting. For northern
European sun worshippers this is Mecca. Anything resembling a
quaint fishing village has been bikini-strangled and Nivea-
creamed. Oblivious to the concrete, pollution, ridiculous prices
and traffic jams, they lie on the beach like chickens on a
skewer — cooking, rolling, and sweating.

Where Europe's most popular beach isn't crowded by tower-
block hotels, it's in a motorway stranglehold. While wonderfully
undeveloped beaches between Tarifa and Cadiz and east of
Alvieria are ignored, lemmings make for the scene where the coastal
waters are so polluted that hotels are required to provide

swimming pools. It's a wonderful study in human nature. For
your Costa del Sol experience drive from San Pedro de Alcantara
to Motril spending the afternoon and evening at one of the
resorts listed here.

**San Pedro de Alcantara** — A relatively undeveloped sandy
beach popular with your travellers heading for Morocco (good
place to find a partner for a North African adventure). San
Pedro's neighbour is Puerto Banus 'where the world casts anchor'.
This luxurious jet set port complete with casino is a strange mix
of Rolls Royces, yuppies, boutiques, rich Arabs, and budget
browsers.

**Fuengirola — Torremolinos** — This is the most built-up part of
the region where those people most determined to be envied
settle down. It's a bizarre world of Scandinavian package tours,
flashing lights, pink flamenco, all night happiness, and multi-
lingual menus. My choice for the Costa del Sol evening is
Fuengirola, a tacky place with some less pretentious older budget
hotels a block off the beach. The water here is clean enough and
the nightlife fun and easy.

**Nerja** — Somehow Nerja, while joining in the package parade,
has actually kept some of its quiet old world charm. It has a
good beach, a fun evening 'paseo', enough nightlife and some
worthwhile side trips (the spectacular Nerja caves and two
untouristed and lovely villages, Frigiliana and Maro, are all within
3 miles, served by local buses). Nerja's beach crowds thin as you
walk farther from town. The room situation is tight in the
summer, so arrive early, let the tourist info help you (open 10-2,
6-8:30), or follow a local woman to a casa particular.

**Almuñécar** — Smaller and the least touristy is Almuñécar with a
tangle of alleys in the old town and a salty fishing village
atmosphere surviving amidst its highrise hotels.

## Itinerary option
To save a day, you could skip the beach and go from Ronda
directly to Granada by train, bus, or car via Málaga.

# TOUR 19

## GRANADA

'There's nothing crueller than being blind in Granada'. It is a fascinating city, with a beautiful Sierra Nevada backdrop, the Alhambra fortress glowing red in the evening and Spain's best-preserved Moorish quarter.

### Suggested Schedule

| | |
|---|---|
| 7:00 | Drive from Costa del Sol to Granada. |
| 10:00 | Find hotel near Plaza Nueva, park car safely with nothing to tempt a thief in it, buy picnic, and go straight to Alhambra. |
| 11:00 | Explore Palace. |
| 1:00 | Lunch in Generalife. |
| 2:00 | More Alhambra. |
| 4:00 | Royal Chapel. |
| 6:00 | Explore Albaicín, view from San Nicolas. |
| 8:00 | Dinner in Albaicín. |
| 10:00 | Do battle in Sacromonte. |

## Transport: Costa del Sol — Granada (50 miles)

The quickest way from the coast to Granada is motorway north from Málaga on the N321. A more scenic but crowded route is along the coast to Salobrena and the N323 north. But the C335-C340 route via Velez Málaga (turn north 20 miles past Málaga) through the mountains (2½ hours to Granada) is even more scenic. Note: the drive from San Pedro de Alcántara is at least 3½ hours. This is a long day. Leave early enough to arrive in Granada no later that 10:00 — hopefully earlier.

Trains to Granada (two a day, 3½ hours) have to go back to Bobadilla. Buses, a much better bet, go eight times a day from Málaga to Granada in only 2½ hours, stopping in Nerja.

## Granada — orientation

Orientate yourself in Granada with the 'T' formed by the two main streets in town, the Gran Vía de Colón and the Reyes Católicos. Nearly everything of interest is near these two streets.

The Reyes Católicos runs up to the Plaza Nueva where the Darro River takes over. This river gorge splits the two hillsides — the Alhambra on the right and the old Moorish Albaicín quarter on

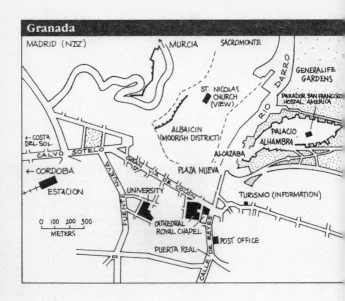

the left. Neither the bus nor the railway stations are central but bus No. 11, from near the cathedral, goes to and from both. By the way, 'Granada' means pomegranate and you'll see the city's symbol everywhere.

## Accommodation

Granada has plenty of good budget places to sleep. The little streets running off Gran Vía, the area around Plaza Nueva, and the road leading up to the Alhambra (Cuesta de Gomez) are all good places to look. The best plan is to taxi from the station to Cuesta de Gomez and take your pick of rooms. We enjoyed **Hostal Navarro Ramos** at No. 21, tel. 221876 (quiet, cool, clean, friendly £6 ($10) doubles, ten minutes from the Alhambra, will store luggage on last day). The **Hostal Landazuri** at Cuesta de Gomez 24, tel. 22-1406, is cheap and pleasant (£7 ($12)). The **Hostal Carlos V**, five blocks from the Turismo, has the advantage of both a quiet location and free parking on the street — right by the police station. (£15-20 ($25-35), Plaza de Los Campos 4, tel. 22-15-87). For somewhere more luxurious, the **Parador San Francisco**, right in the Alhambra, is Spain's most expensive parador and well worth it. It's a serene palace itself complete with gardens and a view. Phone ahead, as its 30 rooms are often booked up (Recinto de la Alhambra, tel. 221-493, £32 ($55) doubles). For a more reasonable touch of grandeur, follow the signs to the same parador and book into its neighbour, the **Hostal America**. Normally, you'll need to make telephone reservations here a week in advance (Real de la Alhambra, tel. 22-74-71, £18 ($30) doubles).

## Food

The best cheap places are in the Albaicín quarter — great food, wonderful atmosphere and inexpensive. From the San Nicolas viewpoint head a few blocks north (away from the Alhambra) to Calle Pagés. Try the quiet patio in the otherwise unquiet **Cafe-Bar Higuera**, just off Plaza Fatima.

For a meal (£10 ($15)) with a view, try one of the restaurants along the south face of the Alhambra hill near the big, ugly and red Arab Palace Hotel.

For tapas, prowl through the bars around the Plaza del Campo del Príncipe. **Chikito** (Plaza General Sanjurjo) and **El Copo** (Martinez la Rosa) serve great tapas but only mediocre dinners. For breakfast have sandwiches, fresh croissants and coffee at **Regina Isabel** on the corner of Calle de Reyes Católicos and Calle Camelo.

For good food on Cuesta de Gomez try **Restaurante El Farol** at No. 10. For a pleasant shady meal near the Generalife after your Alhambra tour, eat at **La Mimbre La Alhambra**. Near the Plaza Nueva, eat at **Meson Andaluz** at Elvira 10 (new, clean, air-conditioned, few tourists).

## Sightseeing highlights

● ● ● **Alhambra** and **Generalife** — This last and greatest Moorish palace is one of Europe's great sights, attracting up to 20,000 visitors a day. Nowhere else does the splendour of Moorish civilisation shine so brightly.

The Alhambra's greatness is really a symbol of retreat. Granada was a regional capital for centuries before the Christian Reconquista gradually took Cordoba (1236) and Seville (1248) leaving Granada to reign as the last Moorish stronghold in Europe. As you tour this grand palace, remember that while Europe slumbered through the Dark Ages, the Moorish magnificence blossomed — fine chiselled stucco, plaster stalactites, colours galore, scalloped windows framing Granada views, exhuberant gardens and water everywhere. Water, so rare and precious in most of Arabia, was the purest symbol of life to the Moors. The Alhambra is decorated with water — standing still, running slow and fast, cascading and drip dropping playfully.

Buy a guidebook, use the map on the back of your ticket, climb to the Torre de la Vela (watchtower) for a grand view and orientation.

And don't miss the summer palace, the Generalife

(pronounced: hay-nay-rahl-EE-fay). This most perfect Arabian garden in Andalucia was the summer home of the Moorish kings and was the closest thing on earth to the Koran's description of Heaven. Consider a picnic in the Generalife. Generalife fountains are often turned off in the afternoon so morning is the best.

To beat the crowds, be at the starting gate at 9:30, skip the Alcazaba, and start out in the 'Casa Real' (Alcazar). Most visitors follow the course laid out on the back of their ticket. You'll do the Alcazaba last and enjoy the rest in precious solitude. (Note: this requires leaving the Costa del Sol at 6:30. Park in the Alhambra carpark, and check into your hotel later).

All parts of the Alhambra are open June-Sept, Mon, Wed, Fri, Sun 9:30-8, Tue, Thur, Sat 9:30-8:30, Tue, Thur, Sat nights 10-Midnight and Oct-May, 10-6. Your ticket is good for two days. Ask at the tourist info about evening tours.

● ● **Albaicín** This is the best old Moorish quarter in Spain. Thousands of colourful corners, flowery patios, shady lanes to soothe the 20th century-mangled visitor. Climb to the San Nicolas church for the best view of the Alhambra — especially at sunset. Go on a photo-safari. Ignore the gypsies.

For the quickest, most scenic walk up the hill, leave from the west end of the Plaza Nueva on Calle Elvira, then turn right into tiny Caldereria Nueva. Follow the stepped street as it slants, winds and zig-zags up the hill. Near the crest, turn right into Camino Nuevo de San Nicolas, walking several blocks to the church's viewpoint. From there, walk north (away from the Alhambra), through the old Moorish wall into the tiny city square. Stop for something to eat or drink here or in one of the many cafes in Calle Pagés, two more blocks north. From Calle Pagés, you can reach Sacromonte.

● ● **Royal Chapel (Capilla Real)** and **Cathedral** — Without a doubt Granada's top Christian sight, this lavish chapel holds the dreams — and bodies — of Queen Isabella and King Ferdinand. Besides the royal tombs you'll find some great Flemish art, a Botticelli painting, the royal jewels, Ferdinand's sword, and the most lavish interior money could buy 500 years ago. Because of its speedy completion, the chapel is an unusually harmonious piece of architecture. (Mon-Sat, 11-1 and 4-7; Sun 11-1).

The cathedral, the only Renaissance cathedral in Spain, is a welcome break from the twisted Gothic and tortured Baroque of so many Spanish churches. Spacious, symmetrical and lit by a stained-glass-filled rotunda, it's well worth a visit. The Renaissance facade and the paintings of the Virgin in the rotunda are by Granada's own Alonso Cano (1601-1661).

**Sacromonte** — Europe's most disgusting tourist trap. Sacromonte, famous for its cave-dwelling, foot-stomping, flamenco dancing gypsies is a snake-pit of con artists. You'll be teased, taken and turned away. Venture in only for the curiosity and leave your money in the hotel. Enjoy flamenco in Madrid or Seville. Gypsies have gained a reputation (all over Europe) for targeting tourists. Be careful. Even mothers with big eyes and pretty babies manage to sneak a hand in your pocket.

**Lotería de Ciegos** — In Granada you may notice blind men selling lottery tickets with nerve-wracking shouts. This is a form of charity. The locals never expect to win, it's just a sort of social responsibility to help these people out. The saying goes, *'Dale limosna, mujer, porque no bay nada que ser ciego en Granada!'* (Give him a dime, woman, because there's nothing worse than being blind in Granada).

**Carthusian Monastery** (La Cartuja) — This small church is nicknamed the 'Christian Alhambra' for its elaborate white Baroque stucco work. Notice the gruesome paintings of martyrs placidly meeting their grisly fates (in the rooms just off the cloister). Located a mile out of town — go north along Gran Via and follow the signs or take bus No. 8. (Open 10-1 and 4-7).

**International Festival of Music and Dance** — From June 15 to July 15 you can enjoy some of the world's best classical music in classic settings in the Alhambra at reasonable prices.

# TOUR 20

## GRANADA TO TOLEDO

Today's goal is to travel 250 miles to Toledo, having lunch in La Mancha country and arriving early enough to get comfortably settled in and orientated.

### Suggested Schedule

| | |
|---|---|
| 8:00 | Departure. |
| 12:00 | Lunch in La Mancha. |
| 4:00 | Arrive in Toledo, get info at tourist office, check in and enjoy roast suckling pig in a restaurant in the dark medieval quarter. |

### Transport: Granada — Toledo (250 miles)

The drive north from Granada is long, hot and boring. Start early to minimise the heat and make the best time you can in the direction of Madrid: Granada-Jaen-Bailen-Valdepenas-Manzanares-Consuegra-Toledo. Past Puerto Lapice, turn off to Consuegra for a lunch stop. Then you're within an hour of Toledo.

Don't go by bus. If limited to public transport take the overnight Granada-Madrid train (23:15-8:00). From Madrid there are 15 trains a day to Toledo, 40 miles to the south. You can take the night train more directly to Toledo changing in Aranjuez. Make your arrangements at the Granada RENFE office in Calle de Reyes Católicos one block down from Plaza Nueva, open 9-3 and 5-7 pm.

### La Mancha

Nowhere else is Spain so spacious, flat and radically monotonous. Except for the red and yellow carpets of flowers that come with the winter rain, La Mancha is a dusty brown.

This is the home of Cervantes' *Don Quixote*, published in the 17th century after England sank the Armada and the Spanish empire began its decline. Cervantes' star character fights doggedly for good and justice and against the fall of Spain. Ignoring reality, Don Quixote is a hero fighting a hopeless battle, a role by no means limited to people in Spain — or to the past. Stark La Mancha is the perfect stage for this sad and futile fight against reality.

The epitome of Don Quixote country, the town of Consuegra must be the La Mancha Cervantes had in mind. Drive up to the

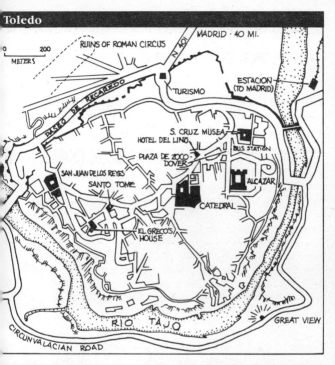

**Toledo**

ruined 12th century castle and string of windmills. It's hot and buggy here, but the powerful view overlooking the village with its sun-bleached light red roofs, some modern concrete reality, and the harsh windy silence make for a profound picnic before driving on to Toledo. In the town centre, 'El Rabaito' serves good tapas and raciones and reasonably-priced menues de la casa.

A desert swim? The fourteen deep blue lagoons of Ruidera are 30 miles east of Manzanares at the beautiful headwaters of the Rio Guadino.

## Toledo — orientation

Toledo's street plan is more medievally confusing than any other Spanish city. But it's a small town, with only 50,000 people living in less than one square mile. Because of its present tourist orientation, major sights are well sign-posted and most locals can point you in the right direction if you ask.

If you arrive by car, view the city from many angles along the 'Circunvalación' road across the Tagus Gorge. Drive to the Conde de Orgaz Parador just south of town for a great view of Toledo from the balcony.

Enter the city by the north gate and park in the open-air
guarded carpark (cheap, but not safe overnight) or in one of
three garages (£2 ($3) for 24 hours). The tourist office just
outside the north wall gate has maps and accommodation lists.
(Mon-Fri 9:30-2 and 4-6, Sat 9:30-2, tel. 220843.)

The station is a good hike from town but easily connected by
buses 1, 3, and 5. The bus station, just below the Zocodover
square is much more central. Buses and trains make the
90-minute trip to and from Madrid almost every hour.

Orientate yourself with a walk past Toledo's main sights.
Starting in the Plaza de Zocodover, walk southwest along the
Calle de Commercio. After passing the Cathedral on your left,
follow the signs to Santo Tome and the cluster of other sights.
While Toledo seems confusing at first glance, this walk shows
you the city is built basically along one small but central street.

## Accommodation
By all means spend a night in Toledo. Madrid day-trippers clog
the sunlit cobbles, but Toledo's medieval moon rises after dark.
Budget pensions are plentiful but scattered, and it's probably
easiest to follow a 'hotel runner' to his place from the Plaza de
Zocodover. Tourist info has a list of private rooms in town. Near
Plaza de Zocodover the **Hotel del Lino** at Santa Justa 9, 45001
Toledo (tel. 223350 or 223354) offers spacious, clean £12 ($20)
doubles. **Pension Sevillana** (Chapineria 6, on the north side of
the cathedral) is cheap (£7 ($12)) and central but not luxurious.
Or try **Hostal Labrador** (Juan Labrador 16, tel. 222-620, £9
($15)) or the big **Hotel Alfonso VI** (General Moscavadó 2 tel.
222-600, £20 ($35)) A bit more expensive, the **Hostal de
Cardenal** is a 17th century palace right at the wall, near Puerta
Bisagra. Quiet, lovely garden, great restaurant (Paseo del
Recaredo 24, tel. 22-4900).

## Food
Eating well in Toledo isn't cheap. But the town may put you in
the mood for an atmospheric spree. Ask your hotel receptionist
for recommendations. Try roast suckling pig near the cathedral.
Several family bars along Calle Nuncio Viejo, west of the
cathedral, serve cheap 'platos combinados'. **Cafeteria La
Catedral** (Calle Nuncio Viejo 1) is also great for breakfast. If you
haven't tried churros yet, this is the place to do it.

For tapas on a quiet square, stand and admire the cathedral's
main portal from Plaza Ayuntamiento. Then do an about face
and walk fifty yards down an alley to **El Torreón**. Toledo's top
sweet is marzipan (try **Casa Telesforo** on Plaza de Zocodover 17,
open till 10:00 pm).

# TOUR 21

## TOLEDO, RETURN TO MADRID

Today we tour Toledo, a city of such beauty and historic importance that the entire town was declared a national monument. Finally, we'll compete our circle through Spain and Portugal by returning to Madrid.

### Suggested Schedule

| | |
|---|---|
| 8:30 | Breakfast, check out of hotel |
| 9:30 | Santo Tomé and El Greco's house. |
| 11:00 | Tour cathedral. |
| 1:30 | Lunch and siesta and shopping. |
| 4:00 | Santa Cruz museum. |
| 6:00 | Return to Madrid, where you have a hotel reserved and paid for from the beginning of your trip |

### Toledo

Spain's historic capital is 2,000 years of tangled history — Roman, Visigothic, Moorish, and Christian — crowded onto a high rocky perch surrounded on three sides by the Tagus River. It is so well preserved that the Spanish government has forbidden any modern exteriors. Its rich mix of Jewish, Moorish and Christian heritage makes it one of Europe's art capitals.

Toledo was Spain's political capital until 1561, when it reached its limits of growth as defined by the Tagus gorge — and the King moved to the more spacious Madrid. Today, in spite of tremendous tourist crowds, Toledo just takes care of its history and remains much like it was when El Greco called it home, and painted it, 400 years ago. By the way, if you like El Greco, you'll love Toledo. And if you're not into El Greco, you probably will be after a Toledo day.

### Sightseeing highlights

● ● ● **Cathedral** — Toledo, Spain's leading Catholic city, the seat of its primate, has a magnificent cathedral. A confusing collage of great Spanish art, it deserves (and we think requires) a guided tour. Hire a private guide. If the £7-9 ($12-15) is beyond your budget, gather a small group to split the price — tell them they need it. The cathedral took over 200 years to build, and under its 300-foot spire (which you can climb) you'll find enough Gothic, Renaissance and Baroque art to fill a textbook.

Your guide will show you elaborate wrought ironwork, lavish wood carving, window after colourful window of 500-year-old stained glass, and a sacristy with a collection of paintings that ranks it with Europe's top museums. All the time I felt my guide's national pride saying, 'Look at this great stuff! Why do you tourists get so excited about Michelangelo and Leonardo? Take a look at Spain!' It is interesting how little attention we give the art of Spain's Golden Age.

The cathedral's sacristy has over twenty El Grecos, masterpieces by Goya, Titian, Rubens, Velázquez, Bellini and a carved St. Francis that could change your life. (Open 10-1 and 3:30-7.)

● ● **Santa Cruz Museum** — A great Renaissance building displaying twenty-two El Grecos and much more in a wonderful setting. (Open Tue-Sat 10-2, 4-7, Sundays 10-2.)

**Alcazar** — This huge former imperial residence dominates the Toledo skyline. It's entirely rebuilt, but its Civil War exhibits give the visitor a good look at the horrors of Spain's recent past.

● ● ● **Santo Tomé** — A simple chapel with probably El Greco's most exciting painting. The powerful 'Burial of the Count of Orgaz' merges heaven and earth in a way only 'The Greek' could It's so good to see a painting right where the artist put it 400 years ago. Each face is a detailed portrait. Notice the artist's self portrait looking straight at you — sixth figure in line from the left. The boy is El Greco's son. (Open 9:30-1:30, 3:30-7.)

**El Greco's House** — Not really his house, but an interesting look at the interior of a traditionally furnished Renaissance home Don't miss El Greco's masterful 'View of Toledo' and portraits of the Apostles. (Open same hours as the nearby Santo Tomé, except closed Sunday pm and Mondays.)

Born on Crete, trained in Venice and settling in Toledo, El Greco ('The Greek') put all three influences to work in his painting. From his Greek homeland he absorbed the solemn abstract style of icons. In Venice he learned the bold use of colour and dramatic style of the later Renaissance. These styles were then fused in the fires of fanatic Spanish Catholic devotion.

Not bound by the realism so important to his contemporaries, El Greco painted dramatic visions of striking colours and figures with unnatural, elongated bodies as though stretched between heaven and earth. His work is almost as fresh to us today as any current avant-garde artist, so thoroughly 'modern' is it in disregarding realism.

**Sinagoga del Tránsito** — A beautiful part of Toledo's Jewish past. Built in 1366. (Next to El Greco's house on Calle des los Reyes Católicos. Same hours as El Greco's House.)

**Shopping** — Toledo probably sells as many souvenirs as any city in Spain. This is the best place to buy old-looking swords, armour, maces, medieval-looking three-legged stools, and other fake antiques. It's also Spain's damascene centre, where for centuries, draghtsmen have inlaid black steelware with gold, silver, and copper wire.

## Transport back to Madrid

Driving north to Madrid on either the N401 or NIV, the roads converge into the M-30 which circles Madrid. Follow it to the left ('Nor y Oeste') and take the Pl. de España exit to get back to the Gran Vía. Trains leave regularly for the quick Toledo-Madrid trip. trip.

*  *  *

That's our idea of the most exciting 21 days Spain and Portugal have to offer. We hope you have a great trip — and many more.

# BARCELONA

Our biggest frustration in putting this plan together was excluding Barcelona. If you're flying into Madrid, it's nearly 400 miles out of your way. By car it's not worth it, but by train it's just an easy overnight journey. Coming to Spain from points north, Barcelona is a great and easy first stop.

This capital of the proud and distinct region of Catalonia bubbles with life in its old Gothic quarter, along its grand boulevards and around its booming harbour. While Barcelona has an exciting past as a Roman colony, Visigothic capital, and, in modern times, a top Mediterranean trading centre, it's most enjoyable to throw out the history books and just drift through it. if you're in the mood to surrender to a city's charms — let it be Barcelona.

## Orientation

The soul of Barcelona is in its compact core — the Gothic Quarter (Barrio Gótico) and the Ramblas (main boulevard). This is your strolling, shopping, and people watching nucleus.

The city's sights are widely scattered, but with a good map and a willingness to work out the metro and bus system, it's all manageable. Use one of the three helpful tourist info offices: in the de Francia station, on the Plaza de San Jaime (in the centre of the Barrio Gótico) and at 658 Gran Vía (near the Plaza de Cataluña). They have free maps and accommodation listing.

Barcelona has several railway stations. Estación de Francia serves France, Sants-Central serves the south, and the Estación del Norte handles Madrid trains and is also the main bus terminal.

Be on your guard. Barcelonan thieves thrive on unwary tourists. More bags and wallets seem to be stolen here than anywhere.

## Sightseeing highlights

● ● **The Ramblas** — This is more than a 'Champs Elysées'. This grand Barcelonan axis goes from rich at the top to rough at the port. You'll find the grand Opera House, richly decorated churches, plenty of prostitutes, pickpockets, con men and artists, elegant cafes, and great shopping. When Hans Christian Andersen saw this street over a hundred years ago, he wrote that there could be no doubt Barcelona was a great city. Don't miss 'Mumbru', a fascinating old Colonial import shop (Rambla de Estudio 115).

● ● **Barrio Gótico** — Bustling with shops, bars, and nightlife, the Gothic Quarter is packed with 14th and 15th century

buildings. Highlights are the great cathedral, the Ayuntamiento (old town hall), several palaces and museums, and the Chocolateria Dulcinea on Carrer de Petrixotl which has been serving delicious chocolate for 160 years — Spanish style (with water), French (with milk) and Swiss (with cream).
**Plaza Real** — A square worth visiting simply for its beauty.
**Gaudí's buildings** — All over town you can find the work of the great Art Nouveau architect, Antoni Gaudí.
● **The Picasso Museum** — The greatest collection of Picasso's work we've seen. This is a perfect chance to see his earliest work and understand his genius (open 9:30-1:30, 4-8:30).

## Accommodation

There's no shortage of inexpensive places. Look around the Ramblas (Calle Boqueria and Calle Escudelleros are good) or in the Gothic Quarter. The best chance of old world elegance in the Gothic Quarter is the **Colon Hotel** (Ave. Catedral 7, tel. 3011404, doubles over £20 ($35)). Our favourite place in a more moderate price range is **The Oriente** (in the Ramblas No. 45, tel 3022558 £15 ($25) doubles). And for the best £10 ($15) doubles try the **Casa del Metge** on Calle Tapinería 10, tel. 3101590.

## Food

Barcelona, the capital of Catalonian cuisine, offers a tremendous variety of fun places to eat. The harbour area is famous for fish. The best tapa bars are in the Barrio Gótico and around the Picasso Museum. A sort of Spanish Hofbrauhaus — huge and always packed — is **Los Caracoles** at Escudelleros 14.

Our favourite restaurants for local-style food are: **Agut** (Calle Gignas 16, huge servings, cheap); **Culleertes** (Calle Quintana 5, a little better); **Siete Puertas** (Paseo Isabel II 14, old and traditional, near the port); the **Casa Isidre** (Calle Flores .2, small, intimate, unknown to tourists); **Florian** (Bertrand y Serra 20, tel. 2124627, higher class); and **Jaume de Provenca** (Provenca 88, tel. 2300029, top place for fish, highest quality, reservations necessary).

# GALICIA — THE OTHER SPAIN

Galicia, the northwestern corner of the country, is like a Spanish Scotland. The weather is cooler and often misty, the countryside is hillier and green — and you may even hear Galician bagpipes droning across the pastures! You're in 'Rias' country now, and everything is different.

Rías are estuaries, like drowned valleys, similar to the fjiords of Norway. but wider and not so steep. Most of them are named after the little towns at their shores like Ribadeo, Viveiro, Cedeira Ferrol, etc.

The Rías Atlas, between the river Eo and the Ría of La Coruna are the most spectacular; high, steep cliffs, relatively cold water, often whitecaps, and great deserted beaches. The Rías Gallegas, southwest of La Coruna, are not as wild. Almost like lakes with much warmer water are the Ría Bajas ( at Corubión, Muros y Noiya, Arosa, and Pontevedra ). These warm beaches are quite popular, at least in July and August.

This corner of Spain may be underdeveloped, but it's one of the oldest places settled by man; the famous cave of Altamira ( near Santillana/Santander) is closed to the public due to deterioration of the paintings, but there are excellent reproductions and original artifacts in the little museum nearby. The cave paintings are 20,000 years old, which is really hard to believe considering how sophisticated they are.

The fertile area here was cultivated and influenced by the Celts, Romans, and Suebs. The Celts left us the ruins, the dolmen and ancient settlements ( Citanias). The very impressive relics can be seen at Monte St. Tekla, near Vigo. They also left bagpipes, called Gaita, the national instrument of Galicia. The people are blond and blue-eyed, and more resemble central Europeans than your 'typical' Spaniard.

If you drive through the countryside, you'll see more ox-teams pulling carts with massive wooden wheels than any modern petrol-powered equipment. This may be more pastoral and idyllic, but the paradise has its price: emigration has a long tradition in Galicia. In the villages you'll find a lot of old people, younger women and some children. Adult men who can work go to Barcelona, to the industrial countries of Europe or to South and North America.

## Cocina Gallega

Galician cuisine is so good we'll treat it as sightseeing for the tongue. It's an indigenous and solid cuisine, and all the ingredients are of utmost quality. In fact, a lot of the seafood served around the Mediterranean coast originates here.

Lacon con grelos is the national food of the Gallegos, a little heavy (good for the hard working people), but excellent. It consists of boiled pork with a sort of green cabbage grown only in Galicia. Along with that you get potatoes (the best in Europe!) and chorizo, the normal spicy smoked sausage.

Pote Gallego is a stew prepared from the local cabbage, chorizo, bacon, potatoes, beans, and salted pork.

Empanadas are flat, round loaves stuffed with onions, tomatoes, bay, and parsley along with sardines, pork, or beef, sometimes shrimp, Santiago is a good place to find uncountable variations.

For your picnic we recommend a cheese called La Tetilla, and the excellent Galician bread. Both bread and cheese come in the old tried and tested shape (tetilla means teat).

Especially along the coast, stop at one of the many Marisquerias, or seafood shops, for lobster, shrimp, crabs, mussels, oysters and so on.

And then the excellent local wines! Ribeiro (red and white) is usually served in earthen cups called cuncas. Watch the red wine, its tricky! The white Albarinho, similar to some Portuguese whites, is said to be the best in the country. The best Albarinhos grow in Val de Salnes, north of Pontevedra.

The Galicians like to drink their own wines, so it's not always simple to buy a bottle of these wines — often they are not even bottled, but sold only in bars and restaurants. One more reason not to miss supper in one of the many extraordinary Galician restaurants. Don't shy away from the best places. You can eat in Galicia's top restaurants for under £6 ($10).

## Transport

The easiest way to include Galicia in the regular tour is to travel Madrid-Salamanca-Santiago-Portugal. Take the night train from Madrid (21:40-8:18) or from Salamanca, connecting at Medina del Campo just after midnight. Make Santiago de Compostela your base in Galicia. Then, from Santiago, hop from town to town south along the Atlantic coast through northern Portugal to Coimbra. There is an overnight Santiago-Lisbon train.

# SANTIAGO DE COMPOSTELA

Santiago, once a popular pilgrimage site for all of Europe, is still a beautiful city, and a good base for touring Galicia.

## Suggested Schedule

| | |
|---|---|
| 8:00 | Breakfast in an old quarter bar. |
| 8:30 | Browse through the busy market. |
| 9:00 | Beat the crowds to the cathedral. |
| 11:00 | Tour the Hostal de los Reyes Católicos (info at hotel reception desk). |
| 12:00 | Lunch. Have an empanada. |
| 1:00 | Try some of the Casa de los Quesos' cheeses. |
| 4:00 | See the Museo de Pobo Gallego. |
| 9:00 | Dine at Casa Vilas or the Anexo. Be careful, Santiago hotel receptionists normally recommend the touristy El Citón or Don Gaiferos. These places are okay but tonight is for real *cocina gallega*. |

## Santiago de Compostela

Medieval Santiago was *the* holy city of western Europe. Around the year 900, a bright star supposedly led the way to the discovery of the tomb of St. James, one of Jesus' twelve disciples.

This played perfectly into the needs of the Christian Reconquista. Until that time the Moors — strong, united, and inspired by their jihad concept of a holy war — were too much for the Christians. Now the Christians had Santiago (St. James) to counter the relics of Mohammed kept at Cordoba's mosque. The legend spread that Santiago Matamoros (St. James the Moorslayer) had appeared charging through the infidels on his white horse. This tale inspired the Christian forces, and it was just a matter of time before the Moors were gone and Spain was once again Christian.

In the next few centuries, masses of pilgrims swept through central Europe to worship at the church in Santiago containing the remains of St. James. (Santiago is Spanish for 'St. James'.) 500,000 people a year made the trek, many using what's considered Europe's very first travel guidebook (called *Santiago in Your Pocket*, or so we've heard). Twelfth-century accounts speak of the plains of northern Spain being covered with people. Today, St. James is still buried there, but Santiago is ignored by the modern tourist boom.

Santiago has more than history — it's just plain beautiful. The old centre; built completely of granite, shines — especially after a rainstorm — here in Spain's wettest corner. This traffic-free old quarter is a compact mix of monuments, museums, bars, and life.

## Orientation

Everything is central: tourist info, bus and railway stations, underground car park (Plaza Galicia), hotels, and sights. Apart from St. James' birthday (July 25 — with a great and crowded fiesta from July 15 to 31) you'll never have to battle the crowds as you would at Spain's other more popular sights. Santiago is an easy town.

## Accommodation

In the old town, every other house has a room to let (lists of private rooms at the tourist info). The best hunting grounds are along Calle del Franco, Rua del Vilar, Rua Nuebe and between Plaza Galicia and the cathedral. The side streets around Plaza Galicia have plenty of hotels.

## Food

The places along Calle del Franco and Calle de la Reina are good. Drink some Ribeiro out of a cunca (white ceramic cup), have some tetilla cheese, almejas (mussels), a delicious empanada (a sort of flaky bread dough pie with meat and vegetables) or pulpo (octopus). The **Casa de los Quesos** (Calle Bantizados 10, tel. 585085) has a selection of the finest cheeses *de toda la tierra!* Ask the proprietor, Don Waldo Blanco, for his favourites. There's a colourful market every morning between Plaza de San Felix and the Convent of San Augustin (Calle San Roque) for picnic shopping.

For your 'Cocina Gallega' experience, eat at **Casa Vilas** (Calle Rosalia de Castro 88, five minutes from the centre, tel. 591000-2170, open 1-4 and 8-12). Josefina Vilas and her two sons are recognised leaders of Cocina Gallega. Be careful, the servings are huge. Nearby, one of her sons runs the **Anexo Vilas** (Ave. de Villagarcia 21, tel. 598387, closed Monday). It's just as good.

## Sightseeing highlights

● ● ● **Cathedral** — This huge Romanesque cathedral with its glorious Baroque towers is the focal point of any visit to Santiago. The relics of the apostle are in a crypt behind the altar. Attend a service here, smell the incense, lay your fingers in the grooves worn by millions of fingers over the past thousand years in the Portico de la Gloria pillar near the entrance.

Until the 15th century, pilgrims slept right in the church. Then Ferdinand and Isabella celebrated their victory at Granada by building the Hostal de los Reyes Católicos next door. Today it's the town's most elegant hotel (£30 ($50) doubles). For those who can't afford the rates, there is at least a very worthwhile guided tour of its lavish interior.

● **Museo de Pobo Gallego** — Located in the Monasterio de Santo Domingo this museum gives a great look at traditional Galician lifestyle. Don't miss its fantastically complex 17th century triple stairway. (Open 10-1, 4-7, Sunday 10-1.)

## Side trips from Santiago de Compostela

The Santiago tourist office can suggest a whole list of Galician day trips that you can do on your own or with one of their organised tours. La Coruna, an interesting old harbour town, is just an hour or two away. The R ias coast offers some unique and powerful fjord-type scenery.

# THE AZORES

How about dropping in on nine forgotten little islands stranded about halfway between Lisbon and New York?

The Azores are flower pots and aircraft carriers in the ocean. Cows, tea, grapes, pineapples, and 220,000 Azorians all enjoy the mild climate. Volcanoes pop right out of the sea, creating a paradise for hikers and nature lovers. Three islands are worth a visit: São Miguel, Faial, and Terceira. The others are very quiet and so undeveloped it's hard to find a place to sleep.

## Transport

The Azores can make a nice stopover on the way to America, if you are prepared to go via Lisbon. Or you can take advantage of cheap excursion fares from Lisbon (7 to 30 days, £115 ($200)).

Once you're there, local buses and taxis serve all the islands. It's hard to drive more than 10 miles in any direction without getting wet. A local airline and a mail ship (the Ponta Delgada) connect the islands. If you have time, the ship does the full circuit in a week, stopping from a few hours to a day for £35 ($60) including a 2-bed cabin without food.

## Sightseeing highlights

**Faial** — The most international island, nearly every trans-Atlantic sailor docks here. Stay in the 17th century harbour fortress, Estalagem Santa Cruz (tel. 23021, £12 ($20) doubles). At Porto Pim, half a mile west of the main town, you'll find a great beach.

**São Miguel** — The biggest and most beautiful of the Azores, São Miguel (225 square miles, 130,000 people) is a good base. It has some fascinating scenery. Don't miss the crater lakes (Lago Verde and Lago Azul) near Sete Citades or the Vale de Furnas with its exotic forests, lakes, hot springs and geysers.

In the main town, Ponta Delgada, you can sleep in the former American consul's old palace — now the Hotel São Pedro (tel. 22233, £15 ($25) doubles, 18th century furniture).

**Terceira** — TWA and TAP flights from Lisbon and New York land on this 15-mile-wide island of 50,000 people. Apart from the large US Air Force base and the pleasant capital town, Terceira is a land of lonely lakes and volcanoes. Daily flights connect it with the other islands.

## MOROCCO

The two-hour ferry ride from southern Spain to Morocco
takes you further culturally than the trip to Spain.
Morocco is incredibly rich in cultural thrills per minute and
pound — but you'll pay a price in hassles and headaches.
It's a package deal, and for many a great itinerary option.

Don't go to Morocco unless you can plunge deep. Going to
just the north coast (Tangiers, Ceuta, Tetuan) to see Morocco is
like going to the Costa del Sol to 'see' Spain. It
takes a minimum of four or five days to make a
worthwhile visit — ideally seven or eight. Plan at least two
nights in either Fez or Marrakesh. A trip over the Atlas
Mountains gives you an exciting look at Saharan Morocco.
If you need a holiday from your holiday, check into one of
the idyllic Atlantic beach resorts on the south coast.
Above all, get past the northern day-trip-from-Spain fringe.

### Suggested Schedule

**By Car:**

| | |
|---|---|
| Day 1 | Sail as early as possible from Algeciras to Ceuta, drive to Chechaouen. Stay at Hotel Chaouen in main square facing the old town. |
| Day 2 | Drive to Fez. Find hotel. Take orientation tour. |
| Day 3 | Free to explore the Fez medina. Evening dinner and cultural show. |
| Day 4 | Drive to Volubilis near Meknes. Tour ancient Roman ruins, possible stop in cities of Moulay-Idriss and Meknes. Drive back to Chechaouen. Same hotel, possibly reserved from day 1. |
| Day 5 | Return to Spain. |

**By Train and Bus:**

| | |
|---|---|
| Day 1 | Sail as early as possible from Algeciras to Tangiers. Catch the 4½ hour train or bus service to Rabat (Hotel Splendide). |
| Day 2 | Sightsee Rabat — Sale, King's Palace, Royal tomb. |
| Day 3 | Take the train to Casablanca (nothing to stop for), catch the Marrakesh Express from there to the 'red city'. Stay near Medina in Marrakesh. |
| Day 4 | Free in Marrakesh. |
| Day 5 | Free in Marrakesh. Night train back to Rabat. |
| Day 6 | Return to Spain. |

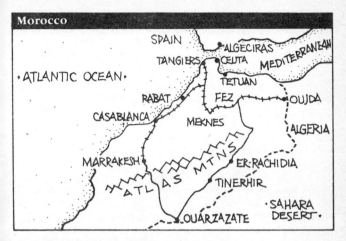

## Orientation (Mental)

**Thrills** — Morocco *is* culture shock. It makes Spain and Portugal look meek and mild. Friendly people, Arabic language, Islamic faith, ancient cities, a photographer's delight, very cheap, plenty of hotels, surprisingly easy transport, variety from Swiss-like mountain resorts to fairy-tale mud brick oasis towns to luxuriously natural beaches to bustling desert markets.

**Spills** — Morocco *is* culture shock. Many are overwhelmed by its intensity, poverty, aggressive beggars, oppressive heat, and slick con men. Most visitors have some intestinal problems (the big 'D'). Most women are harrassed on the streets by randy but generally harmless men. Things don't work smoothly. In fact, after Morocco, Spain resembles Sweden for efficiency. The language barrier is a problem since French, not English, is Morocco's second language, and most English-speaking Moroccans the tourist meets are con men.

## Transport

Sailing from Spain to Morocco is cheap and easy (two hours, £3.50 ($6)/person, £18-25 ($30-40)/vehicle, no reservations needed, ten boats a day). No vaccinations are necessary. If possible, buy a return ticket from Spain. We've had departures from Morocco delayed by ticket-buying hassles there. Change money upon arrival only at a bank. (Banks have uniform rates. The black market is dangerous.) Change only what you need and keep the bank receipt to reconvert if necessary. Don't leave the country with Moroccan money.

Those driving cars should sail to Ceuta, a Spanish possession (ten crossings a day from Algeciras). Crossing the border is a bit unnerving since you'll be hustled through several bureaucratic hoops. You'll go through customs, buy Moroccan insurance for your car (cheap and easy) and really feel at the mercy of a bristly bunch of shady-looking people you'd rather not be at the mercy of. Most cars are shepherded through by a guy who will expect a tip. Relax, let him grease those customs wheels. He's worth a tip. As soon as possible, hit the road and drive to Chechaouen — the best first stop for those driving.

Those relying on public transport should sail to Tangiers. Blast your way through customs, listen to no shark who tells you there's no way out until tomorrow, and walk from the boat dock over to the station. From there just set your sights on Rabat. Make Rabat, a dignified European-type town without the sharks, your get-acquainted stop in Morocco. From there trains will take you farther south.

Moroccan trains are quite good. Second class is cheap and comfortable. There are only two lines: Oujda-Fez-Meknes-Rabat-Casablanca (seven times a day), and Tangiers-Rabat-Casablanca-Marrakesh (three trains daily).

## Sightseeing highlights — Moroccan towns

**Chechaouen** — The first pleasant town beyond the package-tour north coast. 90 minutes by bus or car from Tetuan. Monday and Thursday are colourful market days. Stay in the up-market old Hotel Chaouen on Plaza el-Makhzen. This former Spanish parador faces the old town and offers good meals and a pleasant refuge from sharks. Wander deep into the white-washed old town from here.

**Marrakesh** — Morocco's gateway to the south, this is a desert meeting place that bustles with djelaba-clad Berber tribes-people — a colourful centre where the desert, mountain and coastal regions merge.

The new city has the station, main boulevard (Mohamed V) lined with banks, airline offices, post office, tourist info, and the city's most comfortable hotels.

The old city features the maze-like medina (or market) and the huge Djemaa el-Fna, a square seething with people, usually resembling a 43-ring Moroccan circus. Near this square you'll find hordes of sharks, plenty of eateries, and cheap hotels. (To check for bugs, step into the dark room first, flip on the lights and count 'em as they flee.)

**Fez** — The religious and artistic centre of Morocco, Fez bustles with craftsmen, pilgrims, shoppers, and shops. Like most large Moroccan cities it has a distinct new town (*ville nouvelle*) from the French colonial period and a more exotic old Arab town where you'll find the medina. Our favourite medina anywhere is in Fez.

**Rabat** — Morocco's capital and most European city, Rabat is the most comfortable and least stressful place to start your North African experience. You'll find a colourful market (in the old neighbouring town of Sale), several great bits of Islamic architecture (Mausoleum of Mohammed V), the King's palace, mellow sharks, and comfortable hotels (try Hotel Splendide, at 2 Rue du XVIII Juin, near where Ave. Mohammed V meets the medina, tel. 23283).

## Itinerary options

Extend your trip three or four days with an excursion south over the Atlas Mountains. Buses go from Marrakesh to Ouarzazate (short stop), then Tinerhir (great oasis town, comfy hotel, overnight stop). Next day, go to Er Rachidia (formerly Ksar es Souk) and take the overnight bus to Fez.

By car, drive from Fez south to a small mountain town (stay overnight) and then deep into the desert country past Er Rachidia and on to Rissani (market days, Sunday, Tuesday and Thursday). From here you can explore nearby mud brick towns still living in the Middle Ages. Hire a guide to drive past where the road stops, cross country to an oasis village where you can climb a sand dune to watch the sun rise over the vast middle of Africa. Only a sea of sand separates you from Timbuktu.

## Helpful hints

Friday is the Muslim day of rest when many shops, etc close.

Toilets are generally of the porcelain-footprint variety. Practice your deep knee bends (novices use a tripod method with one hand on the back wall) and carry toilet paper with you.

Hashish (kif) is popular but illegal in Morocco as many foreigners in local jails would love to remind you. Many who sell it cheap make their profit after you get arrested. Cars and buses are stopped and checked by police routinely throughout Morocco — especially in the Chechaouen region, Morocco's kif capital.

Bring good info with you from home or Spain. The *Let's Go: Spain, Portugal and Morocco* book is indispensable. If you read French the green Michelin *Morocco* guidebook is also great. Buy the best map you can find locally — names are always changing and it's helpful to have towns, roads, etc down in Arabic.

If driving, never rely on the oncoming driver's skill. Drive very defensively. Night driving is dangerous. Pay a guard to watch your car overnight.

While Moroccans are some of Africa's wealthiest people, you are still incredibly rich to them. This imbalance causes predictable problems. Wear your moneybelt, don't be a sucker to clever local con artists, and haggle when appropriate — prices skyrocket for tourists.

You'll attract sharks like flies at every famous tourist sight. They will lie to you, get you lost, blackmail you, and pester you. Never leave your car or baggage where you can't get back to it without your 'guide'. Anything you buy in their company gets them a 20-30% commission. Normally, locals, shopkeepers, and police will come to your rescue when the shark's heat becomes unbearable. We usually hire young kids as guides, since once you're 'taken' the rest leave you alone.

Navigate the labyrinthine medinas by altitude, gates, and famous mosques, towers or buildings. Write down what gate you came in by so you can enjoy being lost — temporarily. 'Souk' is Arabic for a particular 'department' of the medina (leather, yarn, metal work etc).

## Health

Morocco is much more hazardous to your health than Spain or Portugal. Eat in clean, rather expensive places, peel fruit, eat only cooked vegetables, and drink reliably bottled water (Sidi Harazem or Sidi Ali). When you do get diarrhoea — and you should bank on it — adjust your diet (small and bland, no milk or grease) or fast for a day. Relax, most diarrhoea is not exotic or serious — just an adjustment that will run its course.

## Language

The Arabic squiggle-script, its many difficult sounds, and the fact that French is the second language make communication tricky for us English-speaking monoglots.

A little French will go a long way, but do learn a few words in Arabic. Have your first local friend teach you 'thank you', 'excuse me', 'yes', 'no', 'okay', 'hello', 'goodbye', 'how are you', and 'one' to 'ten'. Listen carefully and write the pronunciations down phonetically. Bring an Arabic phrasebook.

Make a point of learning the local number symbols; they are not like ours (which we call 'Arabic'). Number plates are numbered with both systems, so you can quiz yourself easily.

Leave aggressive itineraries and split-second timing for Germans. Morocco must be taken on its own terms. In Morocco things go smoothly only '*In Sha Allah*' — if Allah so wills.

# IBERIAN HISTORY

The cultural landscape of present-day Spain and Portugal was shaped by the various civilisations who conquered and settled on the peninsula. Iberia's warm and sunny weather and fertile soil attracted all early Mediterranean peoples.

The Greeks came to Cádiz around 1100 BC, followed by the Romans, who occupied the country for almost 1,000 years until 400 AD. The Roman influence carried on long after the Empire crumbled: cultural values, materials and building techniques, even Roman-style farming equipment, which was used well into the 9th century. And, of course, wine.

## Moors

The Moors, North Africans of the Islamic faith who occupied Spain, had the greatest cultural influence on Spanish and Portuguese history. They arrived on the Rock of Gibraltar in 711 AD and moved north. In the incredibly short time of seven years the Moors completely conquered the peninsula.

They established their power and Moslem culture — but in a soft way. Non-Moslems were tolerated and often rose to positions of wealth and power. Instead of blindly suppressing the natives by force, the Moors used their superior power and knowledge to develop whatever they found. For example, they even encouraged the growing of wine although they themselves weren't allowed to drink alcohol for religious reasons.

The Moors ruled for more than 700 years (711-1492). Throughout that time, pockets of Christianity remained. Local Christian kings fought against the Moors whenever they could, whittling away at the Moslem empire, gaining more and more land. The last Moorish stronghold, Granada, fell to the Christians in 1492.

The slow process of the 'Reconquista' (re-conquest) formed the two independent states of Portugal and Spain. In 1139 Alfonso Henriques beat the Moors near present-day Beja, southern Portugal, and proclaimed himself king of the area. By 1200 the state of Portugal already had the same borders as today — making it the oldest unchanged state in Europe. The rest of the peninsula was a loosely-knit collection of smaller kingdoms until 1469, when Fernando II of Aragon married Isabel of Castilla (the 'Catholic Monarchs'), uniting the other kingdoms under their rule.

## The Golden Age

The expulsion of the Moors set the stage for the rise of Portugal and Spain as naval powers and colonial superpowers — the Golden Age! The Spaniards, fuelled by the religious fervour of their Reconquista of the Moslems, were interested in spreading Christianity to the newly discovered New World. Wherever they landed they tried to Christianise the natives— with the sword, if necessary.

The Portuguese expansion was motivated more by economic concerns. Their excursions overseas were planned, cool, and rational. They colonised the nearby coasts of Africa first, progressing slowly to Asia and South America.

Through exploration (and exploitation) of the colonies, tremendous amounts of gold came into each country. Art and courtly life developed fast in this Golden Age. Aristocracy and clergy were swimming in money.

In Portugal the fairy-tale architecture of the Manueline style developed. In Spain, El Escorial is a monument of power— anyone building such a monstrous edifice must have believed his power to be eternal.

The French Baroque architecture that you'll see (eg La Granja and the Royal Palace in Madrid) is a reminder that Spain was ruled by the French Bourbon family in the 18th century.

## Slow decline

The fast money from the colonies kept them from seeing the dangers at home. Great Britain and the Netherlands also were becoming naval powers, defeating the Spanish Armada in 1588. The Portuguese imported everything, didn't grow their own wheat anymore and neglected their fields.

During the centuries when science and technology in all other European countries developed as never before, Spain and Portugal were occupied with their failed colonial politics.

Endless battles, wars of succession, revolutions and counter-revolutions weakened the countries. In this chaos, there was no chance to develop democratic forms of life. Dictators in both countries made the rich richer and kept the masses under-privileged.

During World Wars I and II both countries stayed neutral, uninterested in foreign policy as long as there was quiet in their own states. In the 1930s, Spain suffered a bloody and bitter Civil War between fascist and democratic forces. The fascist dictator Franco prevailed, ruling the country until his death in the 1970s.

Democracy in Spain and Portugal is still young. After an unbloody revolution, Portugal held democratic elections in 1975. Spain, after 41 years of dictatorship, had elections in 1977.

Today, socialists are in power in both countries. They've adopted a policy of balance to save the young democracies and fight problems like unemployment and foreign debts— with moderate success. Recently they joined the European Economic Community.

# ART AND ARCHITECTURE

## Architecture

The two most fertile periods of architectural innovation in Spain and Portugal were the Moorish occupation and the Golden Age. Otherwise, Spanish architecture follows many of the same trends as the rest of Europe.

The Moors (700-1500) brought Middle-Eastern styles with them, such as the horseshoe arch, minarets, and floor plans designed for mosques. Islam forbids the sculpting or painting of human or animal figures ('graven images'), so artists expressed their creativity with elaborate geometric patterns. The ornate stucco of the Alhambra, the striped arches of Cordoba's mosque, and decorative coloured tiles are evidence of the Moorish sense of beauty. Mozarabic and Mudejar styles blended Islamic and Christian elements.

As the Christians slowly reconquered the country, they turned their fervour into stone, building churches in both the heavy fortress-of-God Romanesque style (Santiago de Compostela), and in the lighter, heaven-reaching, stained-glass Gothic style (Barcelona, Toledo, Seville). Gothic was an import from France, trickling into conservative Spain long after it swept through Europe.

The money reaped and raped from Spain's colonies in the Golden Age (1500-1650) spurred new construction. Churches and palaces were built using the solid, geometrical style of the Italian Renaissance (El Escorial) and the more ornamented Baroque. Ornamentation reached unprecedented heights in Spain, culminating in the Plateresque style of stonework, so called because it resembles intricate silver filigree work.

In Portugal, the highly ornamented style is called Manueline. The Belem monastery in Lisbon is its best example.

After the Golden Age, innovation in both countries died out, and most buildings from the 18th and 19th centuries follow predictable European lines.

Spain's major contribution to modern architecture is the Art Nouveau work of Antoni Gaudi early in this century. Many of his 'cake-left-out-in-the-rain' buildings, with their asymmetrical designs and sinuous lines, can be found in Barcelona.

## Art

The 'Big Three' in Spanish painting are El Greco, Velázquez, and Goya.

**El Greco** (1541-1614) exemplifies the spiritual fervour of so much Spanish art. The drama, the surreal colours, and the intentionally unnatural distortion have the intensity of a religious vision.

**Diego Velázquez** ( 1599-1660 ) went to the opposite extreme. His masterful court portraits are studies in realism and cool detachment from his subjects.

**Goya** ( 1746-1828 ) matched Velázquez's technique, but not his detachment. He let his liberal tendencies shine through in unflattering portraits of royalty and in emotional scenes of abuse of power. He unleashed his inner passions in the eerie nightmarish canvases of his last, 'dark' stage.

In this century, **Pablo Picasso** ( don't miss his mural, *Guernica*), the surrealist **Salvador Dali**, and **Joan Miro** have made their marks.

## History and Art Terms

**Alcazaba**   Moorish castle
**Alcazar**   initially a Moorish fortified castle, later a residence
**Ayuntamiento**   town hall
**Azulejo**   blue or coloured tiles
**Feria**   fair
**Inquisition**   religious and civil courts begun in the Middle Ages for trying heretics and sinners. Punishment ranged from prayer to imprisonment, torture and death. An estimated 2,000 heretics were burned at the stake during the reign of one notorious Grand Inquisitor.
**Moros**   Moors. Moslem people from North Africa.
**Moriscos**   Moors converted to Christianity after the victory of the Catholics.
**Mozarabs**   Christians under Moorish rule.

# BULLFIGHTING

The bullfight is as much a ritual as it is a sport, so while no two bullfights are the same, they unfold along a strict pattern.

The ceremony begins punctually with a parade of participants around the ring. Then the trumpet sounds, the 'Gate of Fear' opens, and the leading player — el toro — thunders in. Any pity you may have felt for the poor bull will be reduced by a cool 40% the instant he hits the sunlight. An angry, half-ton animal is an awesome sight even from the cheap seats.

The fight is divided into three acts. The first is designed to size the bull up and wear him down. The matador, with help from his assistants, attracts the bull with the shake of the cape, then directs him past his body, as close as his bravery allows. After a few passes, the picadors enter mounted on horseback to spear the powerful swollen lump of muscle at the back of the bull's neck. This lowers the bull's head and weakens the thrust of his horns.

In the second, the matador's assistants (banderilleros) continue to enrage and weaken the bull. The unarmed banderillero charges the charging bull and, leaping acrobatically across the bull's path, plunges brightly coloured barbed sticks into the bull's vital neck muscle.

After a short intermission, during which the matador may, according to tradition, ask permission to kill the bull and dedicate the kill to someone in the crowd, the final, lethal act begins.

The matador tries to dominate and tire the bull with hypnotic capework. A good pass is when the matador stands completely still while the bull charges past. Then the matador thrusts a sword between the animal's shoulderblades for the kill. A quick kill is not always easy, and the matador may have to make several bloody thrusts before the sword stays in.

Throughout the fight, the crowd shows its approval or impatience. Shouts of 'Ole!' or 'Torero!' means they like what they see — whistling or rhythmic hand clapping greets cowardice and incompetence.

After an exceptional fight, the crowd may wave white handkerchiefs to ask that the matador be awarded the bull's ear or tail. A brave bull — though dead — gets a victory lap from the mule team on his way to the slaughterhouse. Then the trumpet sounds, and a new bull enters to face a fresh matador.

For a closer look at bullfighting, read Hemingway's classic *Death in the Afternoon.*

# SPANISH CUISINE

Spaniards eat to live, not vice versa. Their cuisine is hearty food of the people, in big inexpensive portions.

While not fancy, there is an endless variety of regional specialities. The two most famous Spanish dishes are paella and gazpacho. Paella has a base of saffron-flavoured rice as background for whatever the chef wants to mix in — seafood, chicken, peppers, etc. Gazpacho, an Andalucian speciality, is a chilled soup of tomatoes, bread chunks and spices. Garlic and olive oil are found to some degree in many Spanish dishes.

The Spanish eating schedule can be frustrating to the visitor. Because most Spaniards work until 7:30 pm, supper (cena) is usually served around 9:00 pm, 10:00 or even later. Lunch (comida) is also served late (1-4 pm) and is the largest meal of the day. Don't buck this system. No good restaurant will serve meals at travellers' hours.

The only alternative to this late schedule is to eat in tapa bars. Tapas (about 40 pence) are small portions, like appetisers, of all kinds of foods — seafood, salads, meat-filled pastries, deep-fried tasties, and on and on. You'll find many hungry tourists gulping down dozens of tapas while desperately looking for an open restaurant. Around 9:00 or 10:00 they are totally stuffed and unable to enjoy a great meal in one of the nicely decorated and good restaurants. Raciónes are larger portions of tapas — more like a full meal (£1.50 ($2.50)). Bocadillos (sandwiches) are very basic. A ham sandwich is just that — ham on bread.

The price of a tapa, beer or coffee is cheapest if you eat it standing at the bar or sitting on a bar stool. You may pay a little more to eat sitting at a table and still more sitting at an outdoor table. In the right place, however, a quiet rest over coffee on a flood-lit square is well worth any extra charge. The cheapest seats can sometimes give you the best show. Sit at the bar and study your barman. He's an artist.

Since tapa bars are such a fun part of eating in Spain, and they have their own lingo and a rather strange line up of food, this list will be a handy tool when hunger beckons:

## Tapas

**aceitunas**  olives
**albondigas**  meatballs
**almejas**  clams
**anguilas**  eels
**bocadillos**  sandwiches
**boquerones**  anchovies

**cachelos**   the best potatoes you've ever had (even better in Galicia)

**calamares**   squid

**cebolla**   onion

**chorizo**   red paprika sausage

**champiñones**   mushrooms

**caldo**   broth

**cocido**   stew

**ensaladilla**   Russian salad (potato salad)

**empanada**   fish/meat pastry (pie) — Galicia

**fabada**   Austrian stew (with white beans)

**gamba**   Mediterranean shrimp

**gazpacho**   cold vegetable soup (often served with fried sardines, esp. in Andalucia).

**guisado**   goulash or stew

**jamón serrano**   special kind of ham. In the bars you can see them hanging from the ceiling.

**lacón con grelos**   Galician stew

**langostinos**   giant prawns

**lenguado**   sole

**mariscos**   shellfish

**pisto**   vegetable stew

**pulpo**   octopus

**queso**   cheese

**queso manchego**   sheep cheese of the Mancha

**salchichón**   salami

**salchica**   little sausages

**sepia**   cuttlefish

**sopa**   soup

**sopa de ajo**   garlic soup

**sopa de verduras**   vegetable soup

**ternera**   veal

**tortilla**   omelette, usually with potatoes

**tortilla francesa**   omelette, the one you're used to

**Bebidas** — When you're thirsty

**cerveza (presión)**   beer (draft)

**sidra**   cider

**café solo**   black espresso coffee

**café con leche**   coffee with milk

**vino tinto/blanco**   red/white wine

**tinto verano**   chilled red wine and lemonade

**zumo de naranja**   orange juice

**agua**   water

**agua mineral**   mineral water

**con gas/sin gas**   carbonated/without carbonation. (Many visitors start their tour hating the 'gas', then gradually fall in love with those tiny bubbles — try it!)

And then there is the dangerous mixture of red wine, sugar, orange juice, lemon juice, brandy and the kitchen sink — 'Sangria'.

## Postres — Deserts

**helado**   ice cream
**tarta**   tart, pie
**flan**   creme caramel
**higos**   figs
**manzana**   apple
**leche frita**   fried egg/milk pudding — that's our favourite!

## Comidas Cocidas — Cooked Meals

After the salesman of the chip maker came through, this machine became the most important thing in almost every Spanish restaurant. But the Spanish language is evidence that there still must exist other ways of preparing food:

**asado**   roasted
**cocido**   boiled
**tostado**   toasted
**estofado**   stewed
**crudo**   raw
**ahumado**   smoked
**al horno**   baked
**a la plancha**   grilled on a hot plate
**a la romaña**   in batter, pasta
**en salsa**   in sauce

## Desayuno — Breakfast

'Churros and chocolate! I suppose if one searched the restaurants of the world one could not find a worse breakfast nor one that tasted better. The churros were so greasy that I needed three paper napkins per churro, but they tasted better than doughnuts. The chocolate was completely indigestible, but much better than coffee. And the great gobs of unrefined sugar were chewy. Any nation that can eat churros and chocolate for breakfast is not required to demonstrate its courage in other ways.'

— *James Michener*
**Iberia**

A typical breakfast consists of coffee or hot chocolate and a roll of some sort. Toast ('tostada') with butter or churros are the most popular choices.

**pan** bread
**panecillo** roll
**mantequilla** butter
**miel** honey
**mermelada** marmalade
**queso** cheese
**embutido** sausage
**croissant** croissant
**café con leche** coffee with milk
**café solo** espresso
**nuevos revueltos** scrambled eggs
**huevos fritos** fried eggs
**churros** sugar doughnuts (shaped like hot dogs)
**tosada** toasted roll, with butter or sometimes paté
**chocolate** hot chocolate

## Regional specialities

The dishes of different regions are as varied as you might expect in a country with such deep-rooted regional tendencies.

Galician cuisine has a cult following, and we are fanatic missionaries of the cult. *Lacon con grelos*, boiled pork and cabbage, along with potatoes and spices, is the indigenous dish. Fresh fish and shellfish, empanadas (meat pies), vegetables, and fruit taste just as they should.

The French insist that the cuisine gets better as you get closer to the French border, and you can't deny it gets a bit fancier. In the north and central high plains, lamb is a good bet. In brash Catalonia, try zarzuela de mariscos (the 'operetta of seafood') or their excellent paella.

Moving south, lash out on roast suckling pig in Toledo or Segovia, and try the fried sardines served like chips found in Andalucia. Andalucia is also the home of gazpacho and sangria.

If you can't get to all these regions, Madrid — centrally located and cosmopolitan — is an excellent place for a 'cook's tour' sampling of regional dishes.

## Spanish wine

We think of Spain as only producing cheap, red table wines, and while they do, they also produce perhaps a greater variety of styles than any country. Each region has its own distinct wine.

In general, the north produces the red table wines. Those of Rioja (near the Basque country) are light and okay and begin to rival the best table wines of France.

Aperitif and dessert wines (sherry, amontillado, fino) are most popular in the hot south, especially Andalucia.

Catalonia produces sparkling wines and brandies, while the central plains prolifically pump out the hearty *vin ordinaire*.

Most large bodegas (wineries) are open for a visit, though it's advisable to phone ahead a few days before to make arrangements.

# PORTUGUESE CUISINE

Portuguese cuisine is different from Spain's but probably not any more so than Andalucian cuisine is different from Galician. As in Spain, garlic and olive oil are important in many meals, and seafood is at least as prominent.

An 8% service charge is usually included (even if the menu doesn't say so) and a tip is generally not expected. Rounding the bill up, though, is a nice touch.

The Portuguese meal schedule is a bit less cruel, though still unusual for the traveller. Lunch (the big meal) is between noon and 2:00, with supper from 8 to 10. Perhaps as a result, tapas are not such a big deal. You can eat — and eat well — in restaurants for £3 ($5). Here's a list of some specialities you may want to try:

**Sopas**   Soups

**caldo verde**   green vegetable soup
**canja**   chicken broth
**sopa alentejana**   soup with olive oil, garlic, bread, and eggs
**gazpacho**   cold, spicy vegetable soup

**Peixes**   Fish (cheaper than Portuguese meat)

**sardinhas assadas**   barbecued sardines
**linguado**   sole
**lulas or polvo**   octopus
**caldeirada**   stew of seafood, tomatoes and potatoes
**peixe espada**   sword fish
**atum**   tuna

**Mariscos**   Shellfish

**ameijoas**   mussels (try arroz marisco)
**satola or sapateira**   big crab
**camaroes**   shrimp
**gambas**   prawn

**Carnes**   Meat (excellent, without hormones)

**porco**   pork
**vitela**   veal
**vaca**   beef
**coelho**   rabbit
**assado**   roasted
**grelhado**   grilled

**Bebidas** — Drinks

**agua**   water
**bica**   cup of espresso
**café com leite**   white coffee
**cerveja**   beer
**fresco**   cold, iced
**gelo**   ice cream, ice cube
**sumo de fruta**   fruit juice
**vinho tinto**   red wine
**vinho verde**   dry white wine

### At a restaurant

**pequeno almoceco**   breakfast
**almoceco**   lunch
**conta**   the bill
**carta**   the menu
**jantar, ceia**   dinner
**pimenta; sal**   pepper; salt
**prato do dia**   dish of the day

## Portuguese wine

Portugal is famous for its excellent port wines and dry wines. A refreshing young wine everyone should try is vinho verde. Since much of the best wine is only consumed locally and never really bottled, it's smart to order the always reasonable 'vinho da casa' or 'vinho de região'.

Branco = white, rosado = rose, tinto = red, seco = dry.

The local Aguardente (brandy) is good and cheap. Imported drinks are heavily taxed and very expensive. With such good local varieties, there's really no reason not to drink entirely local.

# ACCOMMODATION

Spain and Portugal offer about the cheapest rooms in Europe.
Most accommodation is government regulated with posted prices.
Throughout Iberia you'll find a good selection of rooms.
Generally — except for the most touristed places — reservations
are not necessary even in peak season.

While prices are low, street noises are high. Always ask to see
your room first — you can check the price posted on the door,
consider potential night noise problems, ask for another room
and even work the price down. Breakfast and showers can cost
extra, and meals may or may not be required. In most towns the
best places to look for rooms are in the old — and most
interesting — quarter and near the main church.

Both Spain and Portugal have plenty of youth hostels and
campsites but we don't recommend them. Youth hostels are often
a headache, campsites hot and dusty, and the savings,
considering the great bargains on other accommodation, are not
worth the trouble. Hotels, pensions, etc are easy to find,
inexpensive, and, when chosen properly, an important part of
experiencing the Spanish or Portuguese cultures. If you're on a
starvation budget or just want to camp or hostel, there is plenty
of info available through the National Tourist Office and in
appropriate guidebooks.

## Classifications

Each country has its handy categories of accommodation. Make
a point of learning them.

In Spain, government regulated places have blue-and-white
plaques outside their doors clearly marked F, CH, P, HsR, Hs, HR, or
H. These are the various categories in ascending order of price and
comfort.

Fonda (F) is your basic inn, often with a small bar serving cheap
meals. Casas de Huespedes (CH) are guesthouses without
bars. Pensiones (P) are like CHs but serve meals.

Hostales (Hs) have nothing to do with youth hostels. They are
quite comfortable, are rated from one to three stars, and charge
£6 to £9 ($10-$15) for a double. Hotels (H) are rated with one to
five stars and go right up to world class luxury places. Hostal-
Residencia (HsR) and Hotel-Residencia (HR) are the same as (Hs)
and (H) class with no meals except breakfast.

Any regulated place will have a *libro de reclamaciones*
(complaint book). A request for this book will generally solve
any problem you have in a jiffy.

Portugal's system starts at the bottom with Pensãoes (one to
our stars). These pensions are cheap (£3 to £15 ($5 to $25)

doubles) and are often tasteful, traditional, comfy and family run. Hotels (one to five stars) are more expensive (£4 to £25 ($7 to $40 doubles). Albergarias are like hotels but without food service.

While these rating systems are handy, they are not perfect. You may find a CH that is cheaper and nicer than an Hs.

Both Spain and Portugal have local bed and breakfast-type accommodation, usually in touristy areas where locals decide to open up a spare room and make a little money on the side. These are called *camas, habitaciones*, or *casas particulares* in Spain, and *quartos* in Portugal. Very cheap, always interesting and usually a good experience.

Spain and Portugal also have luxurious government sponsored historic inns. These *paradores* (Spain) and *pousadas* (Portugal) are often renovated castles, palaces and monasteries, many with great views and incredible atmosphere. Always great value, their prices range from £15 to £30 ($25 to $50) per double. *Pousadas* have a reputation for serving fine food while the *paradores* are often disappointing in this respect. The *paradores* of central and northern Spain are usually better than Mediterranean ones. Reservations are a good idea at any time and are virtually required in the summer. The receptionists usually speak English and are happy to phone the next one to make a reservation for you.

There is plenty of info on these places both from the National Tourist Offices and in guidebooks. For information on *pousadas*, write to ENATUR/Avda. Santa Joana Princesa 10A/Lisbon (tel. 889078).

# TRANSPORT

Public transport on the Iberian Peninsula is generally slower, less frequent and less efficient than in northern Europe. The one saving grace is that it's cheaper.

Train fares are calculated by the kilometre. Second-class trains charge 33ptas/10km, while first-class charges 50ptas/10km. Faster trains (Talgo, Inter-City, Ter, and Expresos) add on a 'suplemento'. Most overnight trains have couchettes (sleepers, called 'coche-litera') that cost about £6 ($10). A 'coche-cama' or private berth costs about £9 ($15) each in a double compartment. Buy these when you buy your ticket.

A 3-week Eurail Pass costs £200 ($350), first class, and would not pay for itself on this tour — unless you're travelling to Spain from the north. It is a real convenience however not to have to buy tickets as you go. This tour uses lots of buses, and Eurail is worthless on those. Eurail travellers must make reservations for longer journeys. It's best to reserve your departing train upon arrival in a town at the station or at a Renfe office in the town centre. Keep your reservation slips until you leave the station at your destination.

The Spanish train company, 'RENFE', categorises its trains as very slow 'Correo' mail trains, pretty slow 'Tranvias' and 'Semi-Directors', fast 'Expreso' and 'Rapido' trains, and super luxury 'Ter', 'Electro', and 'Talgo' trains. These get more expensive as they pick up speed, but all are much cheaper than their northern European counterparts.

Portugal doesn't have the same categories as Spain — mostly just slow milk-run trains and an occasional *expresso*.

Since trains in Spain are nearly always late, telephone the stations to confirm departure times. Remember, you may arrive an hour after a train has left — according to the schedule — and still catch it. Use these railway info numbers:

**Barcelona** — 250-4235, or 250-4110
**Granada** — 223119, or 223497
**Madrid** — 222-5998, 222-1961, 222-9328, or 247-0000
**Málaga** — 213122 or 214127
**Salamanca** — 212454 or 221224
**Seville** — 222693 or 217998
**Toledo** — 221272

For the complete schedule and explanation of the Spanish train system, pick up the 'Grandes Relaciones Guía Renfe', available for 50p ($1) at any station. The 'Trenes Entre Ciudades' is shorter, free and easier to find. When reading schedules, remember: in

Spain 'Salidas' means departures, 'Llegadas' is arrivals; in
Portugal 'Partidas' and 'Chegadas' are departures and arrivals.

Buses will take you where the trains don't — your best bet for
small towns. They vary a lot in speed, and are at least as cheap
as the trains (60p ($1) per 20 miles). Remember, public
transport on Sundays and holidays is greatly reduced.

In Portugal, 'Paragem' = bus stop. In the countryside, stop
buses by waving.

Taxis are very cheap everywhere. Use them, but insist on the
meter.

Driving in Iberia is great, although major roads can be clogged
by endless caravans of slow moving trucks. Car hire is as cheap
as anywhere in Europe — £75 ($130)/week with unlimited
mileage through your travel agent or on the spot over there. All
you need is your driver's licence. Remember, drive very
defensively. If you have an accident, you'll be blamed and are in
for a monumental headache. Seat belts are required by law.
Petrol and diesel prices are controlled and the same everywhere.
In Iberia 'gasolina' is either 'normal' or 'super'. Diesel is 'gasoleo'.
Petrol will cost you around £2 ($3) per gallon. Diesel is cheaper
than petrol. Expect to be stopped by the police for a routine
check. (Be sure your car insurance form is up to date.)

## Parking

Choose a parking place carefully and never leave valuables in the
car. You'll hear parking attendants constantly warning people,
'Nada en el coche!' — Nothing in the car!

Privacy is a rare commodity for the Romeos and Juliets of
Spain and Portugal. With so many very crowded apartments,
young Iberian lovers can only 'borrow the car'. Outside any big
city you'll find viewpoints and any romantic parking place
clogged with steamy windowed Spanish-made Fiats nearly every
night. Not a good place for sightseeing.

## From England to Spain

If you're travelling from London to Madrid, a charter plane ticket
can get you there for the price of a train ticket and for half the
price of a regular air ticket. One-way flights on Dan-Air cost
about £80 ($140) and can be purchased quite easily in London.
Newspapers list special deals in the classified section.

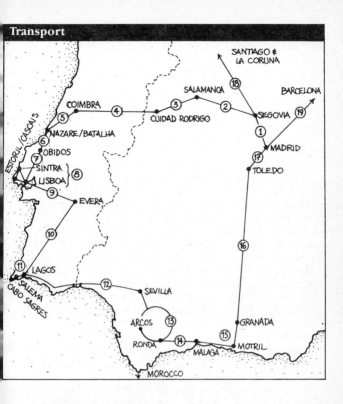

## Transport segments

1.  Madrid-Segovia ( 50 mls )
2.  Segovia-Salamanca ( 100 mls )
3.  Salamanca-Ciudad Rodrigo ( 60 mls )
4.  Ciudad Rodrigo-Coimbra ( 150 mls )
5.  Coimbra-Batalha-Nazare/São Martinho ( 60 mls )
6.  Nazare-Obidos ( 30 mls )
7.  Obidos-Lisbon ( 30 mls )
8.  Lisbon-Sintra-Capo da Roca-Cascaís-Lisbon ( 70 mls )
9.  Lisbon-Evora ( 90 mls )
10. Evora-Lagos/Algarve ( 150 mls )
11. Excursion: Salema-Cape Sagres-Salema ( 50 mls )
12. Algarve-Seville ( 150 mls )
13. Seville-Andalucia-Ronda ( As many miles as you like )
14. Ronda-Costa del Sol ( 40 mls )
15. Costa del Sol-Granada ( 50 mls )

16.     Granada-Toledo ( 250 mls )
17.     Toledo-Madrid ( 40 mls )
18.     Post-Tour: Madrid-Galicia ( 400 mls, 300 by plane )
19.     Post-Tour: Madrid-Barcelona ( 400 mls, 300 by plane )

# LANGUAGE

Spanish is one of the Romance languages — from Roman Latin — along with Portuguese, French, and Italian. Knowing any one of these helps with some basic Spanish phrases.

Spanish nouns have gender. There are masculine words, generally ending in 'o' and feminine words ending in 'a' or 'ion'. The adjectives that describe them must change spelling to match these endings.

## Pronunciation

You pronounce Spanish pretty much as it's spelled. Don't 'cheat' by slipping into standard English sloppiness. *Peseta* should be Pay-SAY-tah, not 'Puh-SAY-duh'.

Spanish is spoken most clearly with the corners of the mouth tight. This should present no problem if you just smile a lot.

Put stress on the next-to-last syllable for words ending in a vowel, 'n' or 's'. Other words are stressed on the last syllable, unless marked with a special accent mark (like 'Málaga').

Pronunciations vary in different regions of Spain. Don't let it throw you when someone pronounces *cinco*, 'THeenko'.

## Vowels

**a**   as in father
**e**   almost like the 'a' in make
**i** and **y**   as in litre
**o**   as in go
**u**   as in blue

## Consonants

Some letters are different from English pronunciation:
**b** and **v**   are interchangeable, kind of halfway between b and v
**h**   silent
**j** and (soft) **g**   like an h
**ñ** (with wavy line over it)   like the ni in onion
**r** and **rr**   trilled trippingly over the tongue
**qu**   like k
**ll**   like the 'y' sound in million

## Words and Phrases

**hello**   hola
**goodbye**   adiós
**see you later**   hasta luego
**goodnight**   buenas noches

**please**   por favor
**thank you**   gracias
**yes/no**   sí /no
**one/two/three**   uno/dos/tres
**cheap/expensive**   barato/caro
**good/bad**   bueno/malo
**beautiful/ugly**   bonito/feo
**fast/slow**   rápido/lento
**big/small**   grande/pequeño
**very**   muy
**Where is...?**   Dónde está...?
**How much?**   Cuánto?
**I don't understand.**   No comprendo.
**What do you call this?**   Cómo se llama ésto?
**I'm lost.**   Me he perdido.
**complete price ( everything included )**   todo está inclu í do
**I'm tired.**   Estoy cansado.
**I'm hungry.**   Tengo hambre.
**cheers!**   salud!
**food**   alimento
**grocery shop**   tienda de comestildes
**picnic**   comida e escote
**delicious**   delicioso
**market**   mercado
**drunk**   borracho
**money**   dinero
**station**   estación
**private accommodation**   casa particular
**toilet**   retrete
**I**   yo
**you**   usted
**love**   amor
**excuse me**   perdone/perdóneme
**You're welcome.**   De nada
**today**   hoy
**tomorrow**   mañana
**hot**   caliente
**cold**   frío
**with**   con
**and**   y
**but**   pero
**very**   mucho
**all**   todo
**open**   abierto
**closed**   cerrado
**entrance**   entrada
**exit**   salida

**free** libre
**left** izquierda
**right** derecha
**early** temprano
**late** tarde
**quickly** rápido
**How are you?** Cómo está usted?
**Very well, thank you.** Muy bien, gracias.
**Do you speak English?** Habla usted inglés?
**I don't know.** No sé.
**more slowly** más depacio
**I am English.** Soy inglés.
**Is there a...?** Hay un...?
**what?** Qué?
**too much** demasiado
**Do you have...?** Tiene usted...?
**I would like...** Quisiera...
**That's fine.** Está bien

## Reference Words

**Monday** lunes
**Tuesday** martes
**Wednesday** miércoles
**Thursday** jueves
**Friday** viernes
**Saturday** sábado
**Sunday** domingo
**one** uno
**two** dos
**three** tres
**four** cuatro
**five** cinco
**six** seis
**seven** siete
**eight** ocho
**nine** nueve
**ten** diez
**eleven** once
**twelve** doce
**thirteen** trece
**fourteen** catorce
**fifteen** quince
**sixteen** dieciseis
**seventeen** diecisiete
**eighteen** dieciocho
**nineteen** diecinueve

**twenty**  veinte
**twenty-one**  veintiuno
**thirty**  treinta
**thirty-one**  trienta y uno
**thirty-two**  trienta y dos
**forty**  cuarenta
**fifty**  cincuenta
**sixty**  sesenta
**seventy**  setenta
**eighty**  ochenta
**ninety**  noventa
**one hundred**  cien
**two hundred**  doscientos
**five hundred**  quinientos
**one thousand**  mil
**six o'clock**  las seis
**half-past six**  las seis y media
**quarter to six**  las seis menos cuarto
**Mr.**  señor/Sr.
**Mrs.**  señora/Sra.
**Miss**  señorita/Srta.
**I have a reservation.**  Tengo una reserva.
**What time?**  A que hora?
**Have you got a room?**  Tiene usted una habitación?
**bank**  banco
**I would like to change some traveller's cheques.**  Quisiera cambiar unos cheques de viaje.
**What is the exchange rate?**  A cuánto está el cambio?
**bus**  autobús
**railway station**  estación
**train**  tren
**ticket**  billete
**return**  de ida y vuelta
**first/second class**  primera/segunda clase
**set menu**  menu fijo
**The bill please**  La cuenta, por favor

Portuguese is like Spanish with a French accent. Unfortunately, knowing both Spanish and French would still make it difficult to get by in Portugal. Our advice is to learn a few basic Portuguese words, rely heavily on Spanish (which is widely understood, though not widely spoken), and try hard to pronounce things like the natives.

As in France, the Portuguese use a soft *'j'* ('zh' sound) and soft *'ch'* ('sh' sound), and speak with a nasal accent. For example, the Portuguese *não* (meaning no) should sound like 'now' said while holding your nose. (Practise this until you *don't* have to hold your nose when ordering in a fancy restaurant). The Portuguese 's' and the 'c' printed with a little hook or tail are pronounced 'sh'.

English, French, and especially Spanish are understood by many Portuguese. And, though you may not be anywhere near fluent, the Portuguese will appreciate your efforts to speak their language.

**hello**   bom dia   *bawng DEEer*
**goodbye**   adues   *erDHEHoosh*
**See you later**   até logo   *erTAY LOAgoo*
**goodnight**   boa noite   *BOAer NOYter*
**thank you**   obrigado   *obree GAHadhoo*
**please**   por favor *por faVOAR*
**yes/no**   sim/não   *seeng/nabng*
**one/two/three**   um/dois/tres   *oong/doysh/traysh*
**cheap/expensive**   barato/caro   *berRAHtoo/KAHroo*
**good/bad**   bom/mau   *bawng/mow*
**beautiful/ugly**   belol/feio   *BEHloo/FAYoo*
**big/small**   grande/pequeno   *GRAHNder/perKEHnoo*
**fast/slow**   rápido/lento   *RAHpeedo/LEHNtoo*
**very**   muito   *MOONGtoo*
**Where is...?**   Onda está...?   *ONder ishTAH*
**How much...?**   Quanto?   *KWAHNtoo*
**I don't understand.**   Não compreendo.   *nahng kawngpriAYNGdoo*
**What do you call this?**   Como se chama isto?   *KOAmoo ser SHERmer EESHtoo*
**I'm lost.**   Estou perdido.   *ishTOA perr DHEEdhoo*
**complete price (everything included)**   tudo incluido   *TOOdhoo engclooEEdhoo*
**I'm tired.**   Estou cansado   *ishTOA kern SAHdhoo*
**I'm hungry.**   Tenho fome.   *TEHnoo FOmer*
**cheers!**   saude!   *serOOdher*
**food**   alimento   *alleeMENtu*
**grocery shop**   mercearia   *merrseaREEah*
**picnic**   piquenique   *piknik*

**delicious**   delicioso *dehLEEseeozu*
**market**   mercado   *merrKAdu*
**drunk**   bebado   *beBAdu*
**money**   dinheiro   *deeNEERu*
**station**   estacão   *estaSAU*
**private accommodation**   casa particular   *casa parrteekuLARR*
**toilet**   retrete   *rayTRAYtay*
**I**   eu   *yo*
**you**   tu   *tu*
**love**   amor   *amorr*
**bank/exchange**   banco/cambio
**I beg your pardon.**   desculpe
**much/little**   muito/pouco
**petrol/oil**   gasolina/óleo
**train**   comboio
**street/avenue**   rua/avenida
**where**   onde
**when**   quando
**closed**   fechado
**open**   aberto
**beach**   praia

**pensão**   establishment not quite of the standing of a hotel
**pensão residencia**   room only ( no meals available )
**pousada**   state-managed historical hotel
**quarto ( de casual )**   bedroom for two persons
**quarto com banho**   room with bathroom attached

# HOURS, SIESTAS AND FIESTAS

Iberia is a land of strange and frustrating schedules.

Generally, shops are open 9-1 and 3-7, longer in touristy places. Banks are open Monday-Friday from 9 to 2 (or 1, or 1:30), Saturdays from 9 to 1 and very occasionally, Mon-Fri 3:30-4:30. Restaurants open very late. Museums are generally open from 10 to 1 and from 3 to 7. The times listed in this book are for the tourist season. In winter most museums and sights close an hour early.

There are many regional and surprise holidays. Regular nationwide holidays are:

Portugal — Jan 1, Apr 25, May 1, June 10 (national holiday), Aug 15, Oct 5, Nov 1, Dec 1, Dec 8, Dec 25.

Spain — Jan 1, Jan 6, Mar 19, May 1, June 24, June 29, July 18, July 25, Aug 15, Oct 12, Nov 1, Dec 8, Dec 25, Good Friday and Easter (spring), Corpus Christi (early June).

## Folk festivals — Spain

Here are some of the more colourful regional festivals. Most involve religious processions, folk dancing, bullfights (corridas) and fireworks.

**March 12-19** — Valencia — 'Fallas' — carnival, corridas, and burning of colourful effigies.
**Week before Lent** — Cadíz — carnival festivities, processions.
**Holy Week** — Cartegena, Cuenca, Granada, Murcia, Seville, Valladolid, Zamora — solemn processions everywhere with images of saints. Seville's is most impressive.
**First week after Easter** — Murcia — spring festival.
**Mid-April** — Seville — April fair: flamenco, corridas, good times.
**During May** — Córdoba — decorated patios and flamenco competitions
**May 15** — Madrid — St. Isidore Festival, a fortnight of festivities.
**Whitsun** — El Rocio (Huelva) — famous gypsy pilgrimage to the Church of the Virgin. The gypsies come from Huelva and Seville along the dusty road either in flower-decorated carts or riding horses saddled and bridled in Andalucian style.
**2nd Thursday after Whitsun** — Camunas — Corpus Christi: mimed mystery play in costume. The struggle of Virtue against Vice; Toledo — solemn procession.
**June 21-30** — Alicante — St. John's Festival.
**June 23-28** — Barcelona — days before St. John's festival: night festivities in the Poble Español.

**June 24-29** — Segovia — St. John's and St. Peter's Day festivals with local dancing and costumes.
**Late June-Early July** — Granada — international music and dance festival
**July 6-14** — Pamplona — 'Sanfermines': famous corridas and running of the bulls.
**July 15-31** — Santiago de Compostela — St. James' Festival: processions, fireworks in front of the cathedral.
**July 17-31** — Valencia — St. James' Festival — battle of flowers and corridas.
**August 1-9** — Málaga — fair, corridas, etc.
**August 4-9** — Vitoria — festival of the White Virgin.
**August 1-17** — Elche — Assumption: Elche Mystery Play
**August 14-25** — Betanzos — Festival of St. Rock: ancient brotherhood dances.
**August 15** — La Alberca — Assumption.
**August** — Corunna, San Sebast ian, Gijón, Bilbāo — Semana Grande: sporting events, cultural activities, corridas.
**Early September** — Jerez — Wine Harvest Festival.
**September 24-28** — Barcelona — Festival of Our Lady of Mercy: corridas, folk and general festivities.
**Week of October 12** — Zaragoza — Pilar Festival: Lantern processions, corridas.

## Folk festivals — Portugal

**Holy Week** — Braga — Holy Week ceremonies, processions.
**2nd Sunday after Easter** — Louie — Pilgrimage of Our Lady of Pity (3 days), processions.
**Early May** — Barcelos — Festival of Crosses and pottery fair, dancing.
**May 3-4** — Sesimbra — Festival of Our Lady of the Wounds (fishermen's festivals going back to the 16th century), processions on May 4.
**May 12-13** — Fatima — First great annual pilgrimage.
**1st Sunday in June** — Santarem — National Agricultural Fair, International Folklore Festival.
**June 23-24** — Braga — King David's procession.
**June 23-24** — Many cities — general rejoicing.
**June 18-30** — Oporto — Popular Saints' Festival: the night of the 23rd is a gala occasion.
**June 29** — Povoa de Varzim — St. Peter's Festival: processions, torchlight tattoo (rusgas), barbecues of grilled sardines.
**June 29** — Sintra — St. Peter's Craftsmen's Fair.
**First fortnight in July (odd years)** — Tomar — Tabuleiros Fair.
**Early July (even years)** — Coimbra — Festival of the Queen Saint: torchlight procession.

**1st Saturday and Sunday in July** — Vila Franca de Xira — Festival of the Red Waistcoats and running of bulls.

**July 25-August 8** — Setubal — St. James' Fair: bullfighting, folk groups.

**1st Sunday in August** — Guimaraes — St. Walter's Festival: fair, decorated streets, giants' procession, torchlight procession, bullfights, fireworks.

**2nd Sunday in August** — Portuzelo — Folklore Festival

**2nd Sunday in August** — Alcochete — Festival of the Green Hat (Barrete Verde): blessing of the saltworks, bullfights, and bulls running in the streets.

**2nd Sunday in August** — Serra da Estrela — Festival of Our Lady of the Holy Star.

**August 15** — Many cities — festivities.

**3rd Sunday in August** — Miranda do Douro — Dance of the Pauliteiros with wooden sticks.

**Days preceeding 3rd Sunday in August** — Viana Do Castelo — Pilgrimage of Our Lady of Sorrow (three days).

**Last Sunday in August** — Braga — Pilgrimage to the Sameiro Sanctuary, procession.

**September 1-4** — Setubal — grape harvest festival, benediction of the grapes, procession, folk dancing and music, fireworks.

**September 6-8** — Miranda do Douro — Pilgrimage of Our Lady of Nazo at Povoa, on the night of the 8th, folk dancing and dance of the Pauliteiros.

**September 26** — Cape Espichel — Festival of Our Lady of the Cape: fishermen's festival dating back to 13th century.

**September** — Nazare — Festival of Our Lady of Nazareth at Sitio: fair, folk groups, bullfights.

**1st Sunday in October** — Vila Franca de Xira — fair, bullfights, bull running.

**October 12-13** — Fatima — second great annual pilgrimage.

**November 11-18** — Portimao — Great November Fair.

# BASIC INFORMATION

## Money
The peseta (pta) is the basic monetary unit of Spain, worth less than a penny. Reckon that 100 ptas is about 50p ($.75) (as of September, '86). There are 100 centimos in a peseta.

The Portuguese escudo ($) is approximately the same — 100 escudos = 40p ($.65 US).

## National Tourist Offices
Some of the best information for planning your trip is just a postcard away. The National Tourist Office of each country is more than happy to send brochures and info on all aspects of travel in their country. The more specific your request (eg. pousadas, castles, hiking), the better they can help you.
**Spanish National Tourist Office:** 57-58 St James' Street, London SW1A 1LD (tel. (01) 499 0901).
**Portuguese Tourist Office:** New Bond Street House, 1-5 New Bond Street, London W1Y 0NP (tel. (01) 493 3873).
**Moroccan Tourist Office (Information Centre):** 174 Regent Street, London W1R 6HV (tel. (01) 437 0073).

## Telephone Area Codes
For long distance telephoning from within the country:

### Spain
Madrid — 1
Segovia — 11
Salamaca — 23
Ciudad Rodrigo — 23
Seville — 54
Ronda — 52
Málaga — 52
Granada — 58
Toledo — 25
Barcelona — 3
Santiago — 81

### Portugal
Lisbon — 1
Nazare — 62
Obidos — 62
Evora — 66